# FREE
## PUBLICITY

A TV Reporter Shares the Secrets of Getting Covered on the News

# FREE
# PUBLICITY

Emmy Award Winning Reporter

## JEFF CRILLEY

 BROWN BOOKS PUBLISHING GROUP
DALLAS, TEXAS

Free Publicity
Copyright © 2003 by Jeff Crilley

Visit our Web site at www.jeffcrilley.com

Printed in the United States of America
Brown Books Publishing Group
16200 N. Dallas Pkwy., Suite 170, Dallas, TX 75248
972.381.0009 • www.brownbooks.com

Library of Congress Cataloging-in-Publication Data
Crilley, Jeff

Free Publicity: a TV reporter shares the secrets of
getting covered on the news

ISBN 0-9726474-0-6
LCCN 2002096289

# CONTENTS

# ACKNOWLEDGMENTS

Thanking everyone who helped make this book possible could easily fill a book. And that's not what you paid to read. But please allow me to give a few people who were key to *Free Publicity* a little free publicity of their own.

Special thanks to my wife, Victoria. Without her constant encouragement, this book would never have been written. Thanks to Dallas and Sarah for believing in their Daddy. Thanks to my brother, Mark, for his brilliant artwork. I will be forever in his debt.

Thanks to my father-in-law, Bob Yantis, for the countless hours he put in on the computer getting the book ready for press. Thanks to my mother-in-law, Dorothy Snee, for her careful editing to repair the English language that I so often destroy.

Thanks to my cover artist and Web master, John Venable, who proves sometimes you *can* judge a book by it's cover. Thanks to photographer Guy Hernandez whose lens should be bronzed.

Special thanks to the people who inspired me and pushed me to complete the book: Michelle Lamont, Jim Halperin, Dana Mayeux, David Hale Smith, Pam Johnson, Eva Parks, Jennifer Snee, Elsie Szabo, Bob Crilley, Oscar Herrara, Craig Thompson, Ken Bradford, and countless colleagues in the news biz who kept saying "Way to go!"

Also thanks to Milli Brown, Kathryn Grant, and Alyson Alexander at Brown Books.

And thanks to my parents, Robert and Virgina Crilley, who taught me everything I know.

# INTRODUCTION

There are many books on public relations and marketing. The problem is they are all written from the PR point of view. It's a case of people outside the newsroom writing about life inside a newsroom.

I'm sorry, but any reporter will tell you that public relations people and journalists often see things from very different points of view.

That's why I wrote this book. After two decades of covering the news, I've seen some outstanding made-for-TV events. But more often, I've seen some so bad it was obvious that no one involved had ever been in a newsroom—or even watched a newscast for that matter.

I figured it was about time a working journalist explained how news works. In this book, you'll learn the secrets to getting coverage from someone on the inside. It's the stuff they don't teach in the PR courses in college.

By the time you're finished, you'll understand why we cover what we do. You'll know how to get our attention, when to call and when not to, what to say and how to say it.

You'll learn how to write a killer press release, how to stage newsworthy events, what to do once the cameras start rolling, and perhaps most importantly, what you can do to keep us coming back for more.

# THERE'S NO SUCH THING AS A BAD STORY

Someone in the news business once said: "There's no such thing as a bad news story, only bad reporters." But I'm here to tell you it's a lie. There are plenty of bad news stories. People try to pitch them to us every day. And you know what? When you give a bad story to a bad reporter, it gets even worse.

So what is "news"? Well, it's hard to sum up in one sentence. Even veteran journalists have trouble defining the word news. But any rookie reporter knows a great story when he sees one.

Great stories have one or more of the following qualities: They are timely. The stories impact people. They're unusual and often controversial. In short, news is just about anything that will hold someone's interest.

In this first section, I'll help you to begin thinking like a good reporter. You'll see why some stories make the news and others get ignored. Soon you'll be coming up with such great story ideas that not even bad reporters can pass them up, or mess them up.

## THE GENESIS OF A STORY

It's not clear who the world's first reporter was. The journalist who wrote the story of Adam and Eve didn't get a byline in the Bible. And no, a reporter wasn't the snake in that story either.

But I assure you that reporters really haven't changed all that much since the world began. We're still just folks who can't wait to tell someone, "You're not going to believe this!"

So for starters, you must begin thinking like us. Once you understand not only what we cover but why, you'll be able to come up with the best stories this side of Eden.

## TIMING IS EVERYTHING

The first thing you should know about the business of collecting and delivering news is that it's based on supply and demand. On a busy day when the supply of news is plentiful, there may not be much demand for your story. But pitch the same story to us on a slow news day, and we are all over it.

## ELVIS TURKEY

Here's a good example. It was the day after Thanksgiving, and I knew it would be tough to find a decent story. Government offices had shut down for the weekend and police departments were running with skeleton staffs. In other words, all my usual sources were home having leftover turkey. My cop contacts, my courthouse connections, everyone . . . gone.

But of course the news goes on, regardless. It's not like we can begin the five o'clock news with, "Sorry folks, nothing important happened, so instead we'll run *Gilligan's Island.*"

There I was, sitting at my desk wondering how I was going to pull a rabbit out of my reporters hat this time. I was just about to light a candle and pray to the news gods when the phone rang.

"Jeff, you don't know me," the caller said. "My name is Shaun Walker and I raise turkeys about thirty miles from Dallas. You know where Kemp is?"

Sure I knew where he was. But I couldn't imagine where he was coming from. "Okay, Shaun. How can I help you?"

"Well Jeff, I don't know if this is a news story or not, but I've got this one turkey that I just couldn't slaughter."

"Really, why not?" I asked.

"Well," he paused, "I'm not a nut or nuth'n, but I couldn't kill him cuz . . . well, cuz he looks too much like Elvis!"

I practically dropped the phone I was so excited.

"Now Shaun," I said. "Listen carefully. You are not to touch a feather on that birds head. You're thirty minutes from Dallas? I'll be there in twenty!" After getting directions I raced out the door so fast you would have thought a plane had crashed.

So, there I was in my nice suit walking through a barnyard with Shaun. "Okay, where's Elvis?" I asked.

"Right over there," he said pointing proudly at one of his turkeys.

But as we got closer, all I could see was an ordinary-looking turkey who was just lucky Shaun had a soft spot for The King. "Forgive me, but I'm just not seeing the resemblance."

"Well, just wait a minute," Shaun said. And then he carefully took that little piece of skin that hangs from the birds beak and he flipped it back up and over the turkeys head. "Now, don't that look like an Elvis hairdo to you?" Shaun asked with a big smile.

I still wasn't seeing it. "Shaun, are we talking about Elvis in the early years or the later years?"

He could see the doubt on my face. "Wait, Jeff," he said. "You haven't heard him sing!"

"He sings?"

So Shaun grabbed both of Elvis's wings and started dancing around the barnyard with him. The two performed a duet for me. Shaun was the lead. Elvis sang backup.

"One for the money . . ." Shaun would sing.

"Gobble, gobble, gobble," the turkey would answer.

"Two for the show," "Gobble, gobble, gobble."

"Three to get ready, now go cat go . . ."

While Shaun and Elvis jumped around performing "Blue Suede Shoes," the photographer and I could barely contain our laughter. It was perhaps the strangest story I've ever covered. And it was so memorable, not only did it air on our news in Dallas that night, but it was also picked up by a couple of the big all-news networks. Shaun and Elvis were seen worldwide.

As far as I know the barnyard pair have yet to sign any recording contracts, but if they gave out Grammy awards for free publicity, Shaun would have one locked up. He received more airtime around the globe that day than he could afford to buy in a lifetime.

I share the Elvis turkey story with you because it's a great example of perfect timing. It came on a day when everyone was still thinking about Thanksgiving, and it happened to be one of the slowest news days of the year. Had he called on a busy day, Elvis the turkey would have continued to live in obscurity.

You see, when there's a lot of news happening, "leave 'em laughing" stories like this go by the wayside. Hard news is just about always covered before soft news, especially when reporters and photographers are in short supply.

## IMPACT

Another thing Shaun's story had was impact. It met the "Who Cares?" standard by which we weigh just about every story we do.

In newsrooms everywhere the key question is, "Will people watch this?" If Shaun had called and said he ate turkey for Thanksgiving, who would have cared?

But the fact that he didn't eat one turkey because it looked too much like Elvis makes it news. Who does it impact? Well, I guess you can make a case that the turkey itself was the only living creature directly impacted by Shaun's fondness for The King.

However, indirectly the story had a big impact. Almost everyone who watched the news that night would agree that the Elvis turkey story was the most memorable thing in the newscast. So it had an impact on almost all our viewers.

## DON'T BE ORDINARY

Why was it so memorable? Because it was unusual. We don't cover the ordinary. We cover the extraordinary. The old news slogan still applies today. Dog bites man. Who cares? Man bites dog? Lead story. So as you are shaping your story, think of some kind of twist. What can you change to make the ordinary, extraordinary?

## HOLLYWOOD HAND-ME-DOWNS

PR whiz Carolyn Alvey took a very ordinary event like a garage sale and made it so extraordinary that reporters were sold from the moment she called. Carolyn knew that garage sales happen every day in this country. They aren't news. So Carolyn came up with a "Celebrity Garage Sale."

She spent months contacting the stars asking for stuff they were about to throw out. Then she put out a press release welcoming the media to get a sneak peek at some of the items up for sale. It was just like any other garage sale, but because these were hand-me-downs from the rich and famous, this was news.

Reporters were lining up to take a look at a banged up Bob Hope golf club or an old softball from Michael Bolton. I

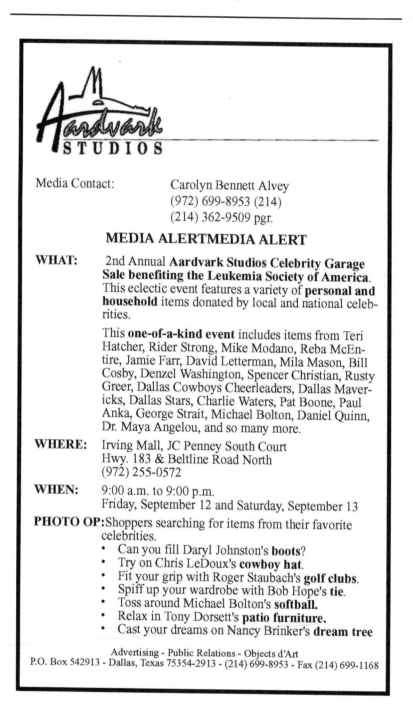

**STUDIOS**

Media Contact:              Carolyn Bennett Alvey
                            (972) 699-8953 (214)
                            (214) 362-9509 pgr.

## MEDIA ALERTMEDIA ALERT

**WHAT:**      2nd Annual **Aardvark Studios Celebrity Garage Sale benefiting the Leukemia Society of America**. This eclectic event features a variety of **personal and household** items donated by local and national celebrities.

This **one-of-a-kind event** includes items from Teri Hatcher, Rider Strong, Mike Modano, Reba McEntire, Jamie Farr, David Letterman, Mila Mason, Bill Cosby, Denzel Washington, Spencer Christian, Rusty Greer, Dallas Cowboys Cheerleaders, Dallas Mavericks, Dallas Stars, Charlie Waters, Pat Boone, Paul Anka, George Strait, Michael Bolton, Daniel Quinn, Dr. Maya Angelou, and so many more.

**WHERE:**     Irving Mall, JC Penney South Court
               Hwy. 183 & Beltline Road North
               (972) 255-0572

**WHEN:**      9:00 a.m. to 9:00 p.m.
               Friday, September 12 and Saturday, September 13

**PHOTO OP:** Shoppers searching for items from their favorite celebrities.
- Can you fill Daryl Johnston's **boots**?
- Try on Chris LeDoux's **cowboy hat.**
- Fit your grip with Roger Staubach's **golf clubs.**
- Spiff up your wardrobe with Bob Hope's **tie.**
- Toss around Michael Bolton's **softball.**
- Relax in Tony Dorsett's **patio furniture.**
- Cast your dreams on Nancy Brinker's **dream tree**

Advertising - Public Relations - Objects d'Art
P.O. Box 542913 - Dallas, Texas 75354-2913 - (214) 699-8953 - Fax (214) 699-1168

must admit, while covering the story I even bought one of Roger Staubach's ties. I figured it was worth the twenty bucks just as a conversation piece alone.

And evidently a lot of viewers saw things the same way. The garage sale sold out in just a few hours, thanks to all the free publicity.

You see? You don't have to build a better mousetrap. All you have to do is take an old mousetrap, say it once belonged to Hank Aaron and people will beat a path to your door.

## No Butts about It

Krandel Lee Newton had the same thought process when he came up with a brilliant way to promote himself. Krandel is a talented artist. He's the Michelangelo of street artists. For a few bucks he can create a sketch so realistic, you would swear it's a photograph.

But truthfully, in the late '80s Krandel was struggling to make a living, until one day he asked one of his customers to "turn the other cheek," so to speak. He began sketching a woman with her back turned.

Well, Krandel took a few liberties with the chalk and a few pounds off her backside. And when he was finished, she was looking better in that tight-fitting pair of jeans than she had in years. In fact, she was so thrilled, she showed her friends. And they showed their friends. And Krandel's been *behind* in his work ever since.

He was no longer just another street artist. He became "The Rearview Rembrandt," "The Duke of Derrieres," or as he likes to call himself, "The Original Butt Sketch Artist." And you know what else? Suddenly Newton was news.

The simple twist on ordinary art made Krandel extraordinary. Since that day many years ago, he's been featured on just about every national news program in the country.

Home   About   Entertainment   Sound Tracks   Testimonials   Clients   Affiliations   Contact Us

**Encore Productions Entertainment Agency**

Luana Stoutmeyer • 972-317-2336

For more information, or to book, call us at
**972-317-2336**

## Butt Sketch Artist
## Krandel Lee Newton

Krandel Lee Newton, the "Original Butt Sketch Artist" has drawn the derrieres of an estimated 150,000 people. He has sketched the behinds of everyone from Alex Trebek of Jeopardy to former NFL star Lawrence Taylor, Danny Glover to chef Wolfgang Puck. Newton has several artists that work with him at trade shows, private parties, receptions and many other events. Krandel has been going full-tilt in the butt sketch business for almost a decade, but is still amazed at the joy people express when they receive one of his sketches. Krandel says of his artists' work, "It's tasteful, it's safe, and it's fast." We would have to add, "and everyone loves it!"

The *bottom line*—if you want the media to cover your butt, do something different.

## CONTROVERSY

We've discussed timing and how to make your story unusual enough to get the media interested, but perhaps nothing gets reporters more fired up than controversy. It's the difference between holding a tea party and The Boston Tea Party. If our forefathers had sat around sipping tea and complaining about the tea tax, it might not have even rated a mention in the local paper, but dumping tea in the harbor created a controversy that didn't just make the news, it made history.

Now, no one is suggesting you throw a brick through the window of city hall to make the news. In fact stunts like that usually reflect poorly on the organization and overshadow the point the group set out to make. But if your story or event has opposition, it's not a bad idea to let the media know.

## CAT FIGHT

Cat lover Bonnie Arnold sure had the right idea when she called me about a controversial new kind of kitten she was breeding.

"Jeff, have I got a story for you," Bonnie said. "I'm breeding miniature kittens and, boy, is the fur flying in the cat world! The cats aren't much bigger than a kitten even when full-grown. But a lot of cat breeders say it's unnatural, untested, and unclear how healthy the offspring will be down the road."

She could have pitched the story as a warm, fuzzy end-of-the newscast story about these cute little cats. But Bonnie knew that by selling the story to me as something that is controversial, it would become more of a hard news story and probably play higher in the newscast. She even suggested names and phone numbers of people in the cat world who object to her breeding practices.

And it paid off. It was one of our top stories that day and, like the Elvis Turkey, went on to gain worldwide attention playing on the cable news channels.

## News You Can Use

- Timing your story will make or break it.
- Make sure your idea passes the "Who Cares?" test.
- Ask yourself, "Will anyone want to watch this?"
- Don't be ordinary. Add a twist to your idea and  make it extraordinary.
- Don't be afraid of controversy. Opposition to your idea can actually make it more newsworthy. So, go ahead and supply names and numbers. If you're confident in your position, you have nothing to worry about.

# THE EYES HAVE IT

### Make It Visual

It's called "television," but many of the stories people try to pitch us are more "tell" than "vision." What I'm trying to say is that great TV stories are stories for the eyes. So as you formulate a story you'd like the news to cover, you should be asking yourself the same question we reporters ask, "What are the visuals?"

### Barking Up the Right Tree

Michelle Lamont of Nixon's Top Dog Gourmet Bakery is a genius at free publicity. I met her several years ago on a story and have done at least half a dozen reports with her since.

The first time I did a story about Michelle, she called me and said part of her business includes baking birthday cakes for canines. Cool story, right? Wait, it gets even better.

Michelle, knowing that great pictures make for great television, arranged for us to get video of a dog birthday party. She lines up everything. She finds a client who's hosting a party for her dog, then takes care of all the details. She makes sure the place is decorated, the dogs have birthday hats and all the guests are hungry. Instant story, just add reporter.

It turned out to be a very memorable piece. Michelle walks in on camera with the cake, the dogs come running, and with the photographer looking on, devour the cake as fast as she can slice it. Another story so good it didn't just run locally, it aired globally.

Michelle may bake dog biscuits for a living, but she'd also make a great reporter. She thinks visually. And that's why she has every journalist in town hounding her for stories.

### The Coolest Scoop A Reporter Ever Had

Hundreds of companies make ice cream. But Dreyer's takes the cake when it comes to thinking visually. John Harrison is the "Official Taster" for the company. He's the head of quality control for Dreyer's and helps decide which new flavors to launch. In fact his claim to fame is being the guy who "invented" Cookies 'N Cream.

But he hardly has time to come up with any new concoctions these days. He spends more time on the road than many candidates do in an election year. On most days, you'll find him in the freezer section of a grocery store posing for cameras and talking to reporters. All ice cream manufacturers have people in quality control, but Dreyer's figured out a long time ago that sending John on tour would bring in gazillions of gallons of publicity. They were right. The press releases bill him as "The Man With the 'Coolest Job' in the Country." Reporters just eat up this kind of stuff. The visuals are awesome. John walks around in a white lab coat with a golden

Prepared by:    Dreyer's Grand Ice Cream
                5929 College Avenue
                Oakland, CA 94618
Contact:        Jill Kasser - (510) 601-4382    jfkasser@dreyers.com
                Diane McIntyre-(510) 601-4338 dmmcinty@dreyers.com
                Toll-free - (800) 888-3442    For Immediate Release

### MAN WITH MILLION DOLLAR 'BUDS' HAS TASTY JOB

Jamie Lee Curtis' legs... Bruce Springsteen's voice ... and John Harrison's tastebuds! What do they all have in common? And ... **who is John Harrison?**

All of the aforementioned celebrities have insurance policies on the asset that has made them famous. John Harrison is Dreyer's Grand Ice Cream's "Official. Taster" whose tastebuds are insured for a cool **One Million Dollars.**

John is truly an expert in the industry, having grown up in the ice cream business (his family has been in the business for four generations). His great-grandfather had a chain of ice cream parlors in New York City at the turn of the century. His grandfather started the first dairy co-op in the state of Tennessee and his uncle owned an ice cream factory in the South. Even John's father was in the business -- he owned an ice cream ingredients factory based in Atlanta. John's ice cream roots are so firmly planted that he claims, "My blood runs 16 percent butterfat."

His subsequent 30+ years have been spent in the ice cream industry, (not eating--but tasting!) and he and his discriminating tastebuds have become quite famous. At 56 years of age, he has tasted more than 100 million gallons of ice cream from around the world. In 1997, he received the Master Taster of the Year award from the American Tasting Institute.

His tastebuds are in their prime. The tongue is comprised of 9,000 tastebuds; each bud has ten to 15 receptacles that send messages to the brain to let you know whether you are eating something bitter, sweet, salty or sour. When sampling ice cream, the main focus of the tastebuds is to decipher the quality top notes and balance of the fresh cream, sweeteners and natural flavors.

– more –

tasting spoon in his pocket. He makes eating ice cream look downright scientific. With cameras watching his every move, he carefully savors each spoonful, like a wine expert.

And John's story gets even more delicious. Dreyer's has insured his taste buds for one million dollars. Now that's a figure reporters can sink their teeth into. And I assure you Dreyer's has covered the premiums many times over with all the free publicity they've received. He's the man with the "million-dollar mouth." But his story is truly a feast for the eyes.

As you're formulating your story idea, do what Dreyer's has done. Give reporters a story so visually interesting they can't wait to get the scoop.

## A WORD ABOUT THE PRINTED WORD

Even if you're only trying to get a story in the newspaper, you should be thinking visually. Give the reporter something vivid to describe in the article. And if the visuals are really good, maybe you'll get a photo alongside that story. Who knows? You may even end up on the front page. Newspapers know a great picture can sell a lot of copies.

Longtime columnist John Schneider points out that many papers, like his *Lansing State Journal,* lay out their cover around the pictures. It's called a patch. "If your event can't fill a patch, it makes it a lot harder to justify putting it on the front page," says Schneider.

Think about it. What front pages do we remember and why? We remember little JFK Jr. saluting his father. We remember the sailor kissing the pretty girl he'd never met in Times Square at the end of World War II. We remember the picture of the Oklahoma City firefighter holding one of the child victims in that horrible bombing. And we remember the rescue workers raising the flag from the rubble of the World Trade Center. Whether it's television or newspaper, the eyes have it.

## A FACE FOR RADIO?

Even on radio, visuals are important. Sure you can show up and talk to the host. It happens every day. But if you have something visual you can bring to the studio, it may help the host get more excited about your segment. And the folks behind the microphones are very talented at describing what they are seeing. So bring props if you have them.

And if the radio station is doing a live remote at your event, visuals become even more important. You want something for them to see and talk about when the radio reporter or host arrives.

Dallas radio host Darrell Ankarlo says the guests who bring things to spice up their segments are the real talk show pros. "I did a segment on self defense and the expert brought in mace, stun guns, and other props for demonstration purposes," Darrell says. "That's a ten in my book, and that's a guest who gets invited back!"

## NEWS YOU CAN USE

- Reporters tell stories with pictures. If pictures aren't there, chances are reporters won't be either.
- Even the most nonvisual story can be made visual if you're creative. Dog biscuits? Boring. A dog birthday party? Now you're barking up the right tree!
- A picture truly is worth a thousand words. And if your pictures are good enough, they'll end up on the front page next to a thousand-word article.
- Don't forget visuals for the folks in radio. Your segment will always be better if the host has something to describe for the listener.

# IT MUST BE A SLOW NEWS DAY

"What are you doing here?" some people will say to a reporter. "This isn't news. It must be a *slow* news day."

But if you want news coverage, you should be praying for days like that—in fact, the slower the better. Slow news days are when stories that might not otherwise make the cut can actually find a spot on the six o'clock news.

In this chapter, you'll learn which days are the best for coverage, which days are the worst, and what time you should hold your event to guarantee the most coverage.

## THE SLOWEST OF THE SLOW

Here's a simple rule of thumb: anytime government offices are closed, it's a slow news day. Roughly half the stories that are in the news are government related. Don't believe me? Just check out today's paper and count the number of stories involving courts, lawmakers, schools, and public administrators at the state, local, and national levels.

It's amazing journalists are able to put on a newscast or fill a paper without them. But you know what? We do. We must fill time regardless of whether anything newsworthy happened or not.

So you, being the smart media master that you are, should time your story for those days when we are desperate for news. When are those days exactly? Just get out your calendar and start circling holidays and weekends. In fact, go ahead and circle the day before and the day after big holidays, because those are usually slow as well. Government officials don't tend to make news when they are winding down for a holiday or just getting back from one.

When you are finished marking up your calendar you'll have dozens of days in which reporters are scrambling to find news.

Most journalists will agree the slowest week of the year is the one between Christmas and New Year. Just take a look at your local paper. It gets pretty thin. And the evening news that week tends to be filled with fluff. Schedule something for that week, and it stands a much better chance of getting covered than during any other week of the year.

## A Christmas Bonus

PR expert Kirk Huggins knew the news would be desperate for a feel-good story when she scheduled an event for Christmas Day. While most people were home with friends and family, Huggins was hard at work helping a client play Santa.

She says a telecommunications company wanted some free publicity for its prepaid long distance cards. So Kirk suggested they pass out free phone cards to needy people at the Salvation Army on Christmas Day.

The event was a huge hit with the local media and was even one of the top stories that night because there was nothing else going on that day.

Kirk's client couldn't have been happier. That evening the news presented the company as being filled with the spirit of giving, allowing poor people to call friends and relatives for free on Christmas Day. You couldn't have bought a better commercial.

## PRIME TIMES

When is the best time of the day to hold your event? It depends on your goal. What kind of coverage do you want? Which newscasts are you trying to get on—morning, noon, or night? Or is it the newspaper or radio you're aiming for? All of them involve different deadlines.

Generally speaking, if you want to get the most exposure, hold your event in the morning. The prime time would be anywhere between 9:30 A.M. and 11:30 A.M. I've yet to work in a newsroom where photographers and reporters show up much before 9 A.M. So by timing your event for no earlier than 9:30 A.M. you improve your chance of getting coverage. Of course, staff can always be called in early, but it usually involves paying overtime.

You don't want to force the media to make a financial decision about whether your event is newsworthy.

Holding it in the morning also gives the radio reporters plenty of time to get it ready for the coveted afternoon drive-time shows.

And these days most newspapers are morning papers. A morning event gives the print folks a whole day to write and edit before the paper goes to bed.

Of course, there are the afternoon and evening newscasts to consider. Generally speaking reporters require about three hours to cover and prepare a story to have it ready for their next newscast. So if you're trying to get on the five o'clock news, holding it any later than 2 P.M. is asking for trouble. You do the math. Want to be on the nine, ten or eleven o'clock news? Your event should be held around 6, 7, or 8 P.M., respectively.

Now, you can understand why I say a midmorning event is prime time. If it's a strong enough story, you may get coverage on all the newscasts throughout the day and evening.

The same holds true for print and radio. The more time you give journalists to do their jobs, the better the coverage.

The only exception I would make to this rule is if you think your event is newsworthy enough to be carried live during a newscast. This is a somewhat risky plan because you can't always predict what TV will cover live. However, if you're fairly certain the media loves your story, there is no bigger payoff than having all the media carry your event live without any chance to edit your words.

### PUBLICITY ON ICE

When the Dallas Stars went to the Stanley Cup for the first time, the eye of the media storm on game day was right out in front of Reunion Arena. There were dozens of reporters and photographers looking for subjects to feature live on their five and six o'clock newscasts.

A small Dallas ice company decided to create a giant Stanley Cup in ice and get some free publicity. When the brothers who owned the company showed up just before the five o'clock newscast with their six-foot tall ice sculpture, the reporters were literally fighting over who would interview them first.

I remember having a heated battle with a reporter from another station because we were both live at the top of the newscasts and both of us knew the ice sculpture would be great TV. The brothers just stood back and smiled. They were featured on every newscast that evening and in the paper the next morning.

Anyone who came up with a creative idea and showed up in front of the arena would have been guaranteed coverage, but no one else did. The brothers carved out some free publicity for their ice business and took advantage of a concept we'll discuss in the next chapter: the feeding frenzy.

### IT's A BIRD, IT's A PLANE, IT's DENNIS RODMAN?

Another example of perfectly timing an event to take advantage of live TV comes from DJ Jason Addams. He tells the story of how his Indianapolis radio station cashed in on the hype surrounding a playoff battle between the Indiana Pacers and the Chicago Bulls.

"At the time, Dennis Rodman was playing for the Bulls and everyone in Indiana hated him," recalled Addams. "So, we got a pair of playoff tickets to a sold-out game, and tied them to a helium-filled inflatable man wearing a Dennis Rodman mask.

"We told our listeners that the person who recovered the floating Rodman when he finally came back to earth could keep the tickets. We knew a TV station or two would cover it," Addams gushed, "but we had no idea just how big a hit this stunt would be. We had every TV traffic helicopter in town following it live throughout their morning newscasts. Heck, they followed it from the moment we launched Dennis off the roof of our radio station until he finally floated out of town and the morning shows were over."

### DON'T FIGHT THE FRENZY

Have you ever seen them feed the piranhas at the zoo? That's what we journalists look like when we go after a big story. We are so hungry we will devour anything that has to do with it. So, don't ever schedule an event that competes with a big news story. You'll lose every time.

But read on, you'll find out how to take advantage of a feeding frenzy and hook yourself some free publicity.

## News You Can Use

- Appreciate slow news days and take advantage of them.
- The slowest times are around holidays and wee ends, so get out your calendar and start circling dates.
- Prime time is between 9:30 A.M. and 11:30 A.M. You want to make sure reporters have enough time to meet their deadlines.
- Allow reporters a minimum of three hours to cover and edit a story.
- Holding an event to be covered live is risky, but for big stories the payoff can be huge.
- Don't try to fight a feeding frenzy. The piranhas are too busy feasting on another story to cover yours.
- If you can't beat 'em, join 'em. Come up with an angle that ties in to the big story.

# THE FEEDING FRENZY

### Know When to Join the Rush

Every once in a while, the media will get hold of a big story and you'll have a feeding frenzy. Sometimes TV and radio stations will devote entire newscasts to one story. Or the newspaper will publish a special section on one event. It seems no other story even matters.

When the media is totally focused on one subject, don't even waste your time with another story. It won't make air. Each station is trying to out "team coverage" the other and before you know it, there's no news time left for anything else. They'll even cancel sports and weather if a story is big enough.

When I was doing nothing but soft news, people would sometimes call with a great story, and I'd have to tell them to call back when things returned to normal.

If you see these news typhoons coming, you have only two choices. You can wait until it blows over and then pitch your story, or you can take advantage of the media madness.

## WHOLE NEW BALL GAME

For example, it doesn't matter how poorly your team did last year, on opening day every baseball team in the country is World Series-bound. Hope springs eternal, right?

Well, a Dallas disc jockey, Alan Kabel, knew he couldn't fight the media attention being given to opening day for the Texas Rangers. So, he came up with an angle to complement the coverage, and suddenly it was a whole new ball game.

Alan sent out a news release announcing that in a show of support for the Rangers he and his morning show co-host would be sitting in every seat in the ballpark on the day before opening day. Pure publicity stunt, right? You bet it was. But you know what? It was so timely that no one could pass it up. Alan hit a grand slam. Every TV station in town showed up to cover his stunt.

Alan knew the TV folks would be at the ballpark that day anyway doing a preview of opening day, and all of them would be looking for an angle. It was either get video of Alan going from seat-to-seat in the 50,000 seat ballpark or interview the head grounds keeper on field conditions.

He had the right story at the right time. If he had tried it on opening day, the game itself would have overshadowed his stunt. Two days before—he would have been too early. The day after opening day? Too late. As I said in the first chapter when it comes to news, timing is everything.

## GOOD SPORTS

Rarely is the feeding frenzy as intense as it is when your home-town team is in the playoffs. I know because it's been "all hands on deck" in every newsroom I've ever worked. News reporters steal what would otherwise be a sports reporter's story, and soon the entire newscast is spent hyping the big game.

## A Cheesy Idea?

For several years, a Dallas grocery store used this situation to its advantage to get free publicity. In the week leading up to the playoff game between the Philadelphia Eagles and Dallas Cowboys, the store would stage a very effective publicity stunt.

It would send out a press release announcing that on a certain day and time it would remove all the Philadelphia Cream Cheese from the shelves to show solidarity with the Cowboys.

The stunt couldn't have gone better. When all the cameras had arrived, eager store clerks would begin ripping the containers off the shelves. The store repeated this stunt year after year getting plenty of free publicity until big games between the Cowboys and Eagles became rare.

## A Rose by Any Other Name

Like the grocery store, a Dallas restaurant also knew the value of showing support for the home team. The San Francisco Rose was hardly an inviting name for an eatery in Cowboys country when Dallas played the San Francisco 49ers in the playoffs. So in the week leading up to the game, the owner would announce he was temporarily changing the name of the restaurant to "The Dallas Rose."

When the cameras were ready, employees would lower a "Dallas" banner and cover the part of the sign that read "San Francisco."

This stunt received several years of repeat coverage until the Cowboys and 49ers stopped having success on the field. And the restaurant owner discovered that a rose by another name could smell very sweet indeed.

### A SMASHING EVENT

Another example of cashing in on fan fever comes comple-ments of morning DJs. What better way for a radio station to get free publicity than to hold a "Green Bay Car Smash" the day before the Cowboys play the Packers in the playoffs?

It's hardly a new idea. Radio stations have been hosting such events for years. All you need is an old junker of a car, a sledge hammer and some paint to give the car the opposing team's colors.

The DJs encourage their listeners to come help destroy the car in the parking lot of your team's stadium.

Of course, most of the damage seems to happen when the local TV crews are going "live."

### GIVING THE JUDGE THE CHAIR

Remember the feeding frenzy that went on during the OJ trial? The media just couldn't do too many OJ stories. So, when word got out that Judge Lance Ito had switched to a more comfort-able chair during the trial—even that became a news item.

The quick-thinking company that sells those chairs didn't miss a beat. Knowing that the piranhas were circling, Texas-based Relax the Back sent out press releases announcing that they were the ones who gave Ito the chair. Sales rose more than 40 percent during the trial.

### A GOOD CANDIDATE FOR PUBLICITY

DJ Rich Michaels says he's never received more media attention than when he ran for governor. The popular Lansing, Michigan, radio personality wasn't endorsed by any particular party. In fact, his slogan was "Party all the Time."

With the media growing tired of serious politics, Rich joked, "I threw my hat into the ring and missed." His comic can-didacy worked wonders. "All the TV stations and papers covered it," Rich laughed. "It was a publicity stunt and everyone knew it, but they carried the story anyway. It was a nice break from all the boring political stories that were going on."

Rich's write-in campaign won him 4,000 votes. He was dead last in the election but won the radio ratings race in Lansing by a wide margin. Rich says that during the week leading up to the election, one out of every two radios in town was tuned to his morning show, an unheard of percentage.

He took advantage of the media's election fever to create his own remedy for publicity. But he didn't have to be a radio personality to win such coverage. Anyone could have come up with a joke campaign to give the media a refreshingly funny alternative to covering the real races.

There are all sorts of ways to turn elections into oddball opportunities for PR. I've covered Elvis impersonators running for office, write-in campaigns for dogs, even people running campaigns for fictional characters, such as Archie Bunker and Donald Duck. They always lose, but in terms of media attention, they win by a landslide.

## PULPIT PUBLICITY

Churches can take advantage of the feeding frenzy too. And as any reporter will tell you, Sundays are notoriously slow. But members of the clergy don't need divine inspiration to benefit from such a situation. It's just a matter of pitching the media a good story on a bad day for news.

Let's say there was a huge tragedy during the week. It doesn't matter whether it's local or national. If the media is focused on one story, you have an opportunity to showcase your church.

Take September 11, for instance. It was such a monumental tragedy that millions depended on their faith to get through. In the days following the attack, churches everywhere invited the media to their services to get video of worshipers gathered together in prayer.

Other churches have done the same thing after big fires, natural disasters, or horrible crimes—events that cause people to turn to places of worship for support.

But it doesn't take a tragedy to get the media to find religion. My father, Dr. Robert H. Crilley, was a minister in downtown Detroit. As a boy, I remember him being a master of the media.

Each year he received amazing TV and newspaper coverage for his Easter Sunday balloon launch. As a symbol of the resurrection, the congregation at Fort Street Church would let go of their balloons as my father cheered, "He is risen."

It was a great photo opportunity. That evening on the news and the next morning on the front page of the paper, there was my father with his arms in the air and hundreds of balloons floating past the steeple.

### JUST WHAT THE DOCTOR ORDERED

Smart physicians can do the same thing. When Theresa Merola-Hernandez worked in PR at Southwestern Medical Center in Dallas, she was brilliant at getting media attention for her doctors, often getting them national attention.

Anytime a high-profile illness was in the news, she was on the phone with the reporters letting them know that she had a doctor who could talk about it.

If the president had a hernia, she had an expert. If a famous athlete or coach died of a disease, she had a doctor who could explain it. Even if it was just lotto fever, she had a psychologist lined up who could talk about gambling.

All hospitals have experts, but her doctors seemed to be the ones who were always in the news simply because she performed a check-up on her physicians and wrote them a prescription for free publicity.

## A Meal of Titanic Proportions

In 1998 the Fairmont Hotel in Dallas decided to plunge into the feeding frenzy surrounding the movie *Titanic*. On the anniversary of the ships sinking, the hotel threw a "Last Dinner on the Titanic" party to increase traffic to the hotel's restaurant.

"We tried to duplicate everything right down to the last detail," said PR genius Gail Cooksey. "From the nine-course meal to the staff dressed in period costumes, everything was exactly like it was on the ship just before it sank. And the media ate it up!"

Boy, did we ever. The event received coverage on every TV station in town as well as front-page articles and photos in both *The Dallas Morning News* and *Fort Worth Star-Telegram*.

And the public's enthusiasm for the event was unsinkable. Because so many people wanted to experience it, the "last meal" was quickly expanded from one night to a week-long series of dining events.

## Don't Wait for a Storm to Buy an Umbrella

Start training yourself to anticipate these news typhoons. It's really pretty easy when you know what to look for. Start planning your holiday stories months in advance. Don't wait until Christmas to get your charity idea underway. If your team is on track to make the playoffs, start thinking about how to ride that train. And never wait until a movie is setting box office records to plan a tie-in. The blockbusters usually create a buzz long before they are in the theaters. The folks who really master the media are the ones who are always shopping for the right umbrella for the next storm.

## NEWS YOU CAN USE

- A feeding frenzy is your best opportunity to get coverage.
- Sell what the news is buying. During a frenzy the news media is on a buying binge.
- Anticipate these news typhoons, and prepare to ride the wave. Is there a hot event coming up? A concert? A sporting event? A hot movie? Plan a tie-in.

# WHO YA GONNA CALL?

Okay, so now you've come up with your own Elvis turkey story. You've thought out the visuals. You've tried to take advantage of the feeding frenzy, and you're ready for the media to beat a path to your door. Now, at the risk of ripping off the *Ghostbusters*, "Who ya gonna call?"

One of the great mysteries of the news universe seems to be how to get our attention. I'll admit, it's not always easy. Our newsroom gets hundreds of phone calls, faxes, and e-mails every day from people pitching stories. So how do you separate yourself from the rest?

The first thing you should do is become familiar with the people who would likely cover your story. Does the station have a certain reporter who concentrates on just business stories? Or is there someone who tends to cover the lighter stuff? Watch the news and take notes. Who covers what?

For instance, when Shaun had his Elvis sighting in the barnyard, he was lucky he happened to call me. At the time, I had been assigned to cover nothing but "leave 'em laughing" stories, so Elvis and I were birds of a feather. But had Shaun called our investigative reporter, that would have been a *fowl,* to say the least.

The same holds true of most newspapers. Some reporters cover "crime and courts" and others "human interest." There are literally dozens of beats reporters can have—politics, health, business, religion, science, technology, consumer, and entertainment. So do your homework. Know which reporters specialize in the types of stories you want covered.

Where do I start? At the back of the book, I've included the Web sites for hundreds of TV stations across the country. Through each station's site, you should be able to read more about each reporter and determine which one is best suited to cover your story. Most sites will also have phone numbers, fax numbers, and e-mail addresses for individual reporters.

## THE WINDUP AND THE PITCH

I love it when someone calls me to pitch a story and is already familiar with my work. If a phone call begins, "Jeff, first let me say how much I enjoyed that Elvis turkey story you had on last week," I'm going to be more receptive to whatever is said next. Sure, I know I'm being buttered up, but it still works.

What the caller has communicated in the first few seconds is: "I watch your news," and "I'm a fan of your work."

Believe me, I've had many calls that begin, "Now what is it you do again? Are you on TV or behind the scenes?" Journalists have egos just like anyone else. Whether in print, radio, or TV, we'd all like to believe that everyone knows who we are and what we do.

So now that you've stroked our egos, what next? Well, often we are on deadline. So if we pick up the phone at all, that's a good sign. But don't assume just because you're talking to us that we have time to chat. Cut to the chase. Sum up your story in one sentence.

If I were the one pitching the story to a reporter, I'd come up with something catchy. I'd describe the story the same way an anchor would introduce it on the air.

## PUTTING ON THE DOG

Laila Ferrell really knows how to sell a story. She runs an upscale kennel, which she calls a pet bed and breakfast. So when Laila wanted me to come out and give her some free publicity she pretty much wrote my opening line for me. "Jeff, you do such cute features. Why don't you come out and cover my kennel for pampered pets? It's the Ritz Carlton for canines!" Then she quickly described the visuals. (Let us know what the pictures are going to be once we get there.)

She told me each six by six-foot cage is completely furnished with miniature sofas, fake fireplaces, even tiny TVs. "You've got to see it," she said excitedly. "These doggie digs are more posh than some people's houses."

Laila threw the perfect pitch. She complimented me on my work. She described the visuals. And she sold me with her "Ritz Carlton for canines" comparison. Now that's good writing! She came up with a better opening line for the report than I ever could.

## VOICEMAIL

Leaving a message can be a good thing as long as it's short. If it's any longer than thirty seconds I know reporters who will automatically delete you.

Practice making a thirty-second pitch before you call us. Start with your name and number. Then sum up your story in one sentence. And you may want to repeat your number again at the end.

But no matter what you do, please say your number

s-l-o-w-l-y. My wife, Victoria Snee, is a TV entertainment reporter. She says inaudible phone numbers are almost a guarantee that you'll be deleted. "I don't care how good the story is," Victoria rants, "If you rattle off your phone number so fast I have to listen to your message nine times just to decode your number, you're gone!"

And if we don't call back, you may want to try again later. We get so busy sometimes that even if we like your story, we don't always call you back immediately. But be understanding when you call a second time. You might want to say, I know you are probably swamped with other stories, but if you get a few seconds, please take a look at the news release. I'll be faxing it to your attention.

## E-MAIL

I've found that e-mail is a very individual thing with reporters. Some love it; others hate it. Some like attachments; others refuse to open them for fear of a virus.

The best advice is, when you're on the phone with the reporter, ask. If the journalist likes to correspond by e-mail, send your one-page press release along with a catchy subject line so it'll be opened. Just make sure it doesn't sound obscene. Most news operations have a policy about sending or receiving offensive e-mails. If your subject sounds the least bit lewd, it'll probably be deleted.

## THE DESK

In addition to talking to the reporter personally, I would encourage you to contact the "assignment desk" (also known as the "news desk" in TV and radio). Newspapers tend to have larger staffs and therefore, more "desks." In newspapers they have everything from the sports desk to the city desk to the editorial desk.

In any event, the people sitting behind these desks are

called editors. Their job is a cross between air traffic controller and short order cook. Typically you'll find the assignment editor with one ear glued to a police scanner, and the other ear on the phone, with the left hand picking up faxes, while the right is wildly scribbling notes. These people have even less time than reporters. But understand—the folks who work the desk can make or break your story. Their job is to assign stories and dispatch crews. A few kind words go a long way.

If I were calling an assignment desk, I would make my pitch a fastball. Try something like, I know you're busy, but I just faxed you a story you're going to want to see. And then sum it up in a sentence. I run a pet bed and breakfast so fancy that it's practically a Hyatt for hounds.

If editors aren't too swamped, they can check to see that they got your fax, and you can offer to answer any questions they might have. But if they seem too busy to talk, be very understanding. Ask them for a convenient time to call back. And get their names so when you call back, you can build rapport with them like you did with the reporter.

If I were calling a hurried desk person, I might say, "John, I can tell you're busy, but I have a story that will knock your socks off. I just faxed it to you. If it's okay, I'd like to call back when you have a few minutes, so I can fill you in on the details. When's a good time?"

## JUST THE FAX

So what do you put in your press release? How do you write one? Don't worry. You don't need an M.B.A. to master this one.

A press release is your pitch on paper. One page is plenty. It's something you can fax or mail to a newsroom in addition to your phone call to the reporter and the desk. We newsies like to have something to hold on to. It's nice to have the facts by fax.

Some marketing and public relations books will give you a format you should use to create a press release. However, as a journalist, I can honestly say it's not the format that sells the story, the story sells the story. All you really need is the "who, what, where, when, why, and how" on a piece of paper along with phone numbers where you can be reached.

And if you are mailing us something, don't spend a lot of time worrying about what kind of paper you use. If you write a great story on a piece of Kleenex, I'd cover it. But write a bad story on the finest paper, and I'll blow my nose with it.

What you say in that very first sentence is much more important than how your press release is laid out or what kind of paper stock you use. I've watched our assignment editors go through faxes. They can decide in the blink of an eye whether it's something we would cover. No matter how carefully you choreographed the colors, if you don't grab us in the first sentence it's in the trash.

John Schneider with the *Lansing State Journal* agrees. "Our desks are perpetually buried in a blizzard of paper," he says. You don't want to be just another flake. And that's the fax.

## WRITE LIKE A REPORTER

The best press releases are the ones with a bold, clever headline as you might expect to see on the front page of the paper. Come up with a "grabber."

I'll give you an example. Let's say you have a snowcone shack, and you want to promote your business. You know your story has to be unusual to get the media's attention, so you dump a truckload of shaved ice in front of your shack and invite children to make snow angels in front of your stand.

You're smart enough to know that July 5 is a notoriously slow news day (government offices closed for the long 4th of July weekend), or you wait until the first major heat wave of the summer (because the media will be in a feeding frenzy about the hot weather). And you schedule it to happen during the five o'clock newscast because you think it could be so big all the TV stations might cover it live.

Check the example below of how I would write the press release.

Notice the catchy headline? That's the type of headline or caption for a photo you can imagine the paper using. And the first sentence? Can't you imagine an anchor reading it just that way? And it's a story so great that even the worst reporter can't mess it up.

---

Contact: Jeff Crilley    555-555-5555
                         FAX 555-555-5556

For Immediate Release

## SUMMER SNOW STORM?

A freak snow storm is sweeping through town. Not really,

but it sure looks like one. The Sno-Biz snowcone shack in

Smithsville is hosting a "Christmas in July" party to help

children cool down during this heat wave. Children will

enjoy the snow while it lasts, which with these temperatures

may be a matter of minutes.

When: July 5 at 5 P.M.
Where: 333 Main St., Smithsville

Of course I just made all that stuff up. But you can see the thought process that went into it. It was unusual. It was extremely visual. It was timed to take advantage of a slow news day or a feeding frenzy, and it was scheduled during a newscast for maximum airtime.

I can't imagine the TV, radio, or newspaper that wouldn't bite on such a stunt. Cool coverage for your snowcone shack, and all it cost you was some shaved ice.

---

Contact: Jeff Crilley     555-555-5555
                          FAX 555-555-5556

For Immediate Release

The snowcone shack in Smithsville invites you to cover

an event in the parking lot on July 5 at 5PM. Crushed

ice will be dumped on the ground and children will be

allowed to play in it.

Where: 333 Main St., Smithsville

When: July 5 at 5 P.M.

---

## THE WRONG WAY

Just so you can see how a poorly written copy can kill your chances of coverage, see above for the same great story hidden in a really pitiful press release.

You see what I mean? No catchy headline. No clever opening line. No tie-in to the summer heat. It's the same event, but it stands a strong chance of being ignored, simply because the person receiving the fax won't instantly see the story.

Don't believe me? I asked an assignment editor from a major market TV newsroom to show me just how quickly he decides whether a press release is worthy of coverage.

He grabbed a stack of press releases off the fax machine and began dividing them into three piles. "Yes . . . no . . . no . . . yes . . . maybe," he said as he ripped through the pile. It took him just twenty seconds to go through a dozen press releases.

And when you think about it, it's pretty scary, especially for the people who wrote them. If you don't grab them with the headline and opening sentence, you've wasted your time.

## YOU SNOOZE, YOU WIN

John Kehoe has a gift for coming up with "grabbers." John is a business consultant, public speaker, and author on "the power of the mind." He consults with companies about problems, and then goes home and literally "dreams" of solutions. That's right. He is paid quite handsomely for coming up with ideas in his sleep. So how do you pitch that story to a reporter? You do it the way John did. Check out his news release on the next page. Can you see why he had me from "hello?"

The press release continues with information on how to schedule an interview with John. It says he'd be more than happy to hear your problems and go to sleep on camera while his subconscious mind searches for solutions.

What reporter wouldn't be hooked by a press release like that? It had everything. It had a grabber. It outlined the visuals. And once again, it wrote the opening line. That evening our anchor introduced the story by saying, "If you thought you had a dream job, just wait till you meet John Kehoe."

## WOULD YOU PAY SOMEONE
## $1, 000 AN HOUR
## TO SLEEP ON THE JOB?

Downsizing. Healthcare insurance in imminent jeopardy. Rents at an all time high. So WHO, in these fiscally cautious times, would PAY someone to sleep on the job? Some of the largest corporations like Mobil Oil and DeBeers diamonds pay international speaker and best selling author John Kehoe to actually meet with them, tell him their corporate problems and than go home and dream for them and interpret those dreams. What do these companies need from a man who analyzes dreams? Like the hundreds of thousands of people, who have been taught by Kehoe, they are discovering the techniques of MIND POWER.

MIND POWER: Into the 21st Century demonstrates how we can relate our everyday lives and dilemmas through utilizing something that we already possess - OUR MINDS. Our gray matter is so powerful, in order to match the capacity of a single human mind, we would have to construct a supercomputer as large as the planet Earth! With this sort of potential put to use, we can solve many of the problems in our lives and, more importantly, function on a much higher level than ever assumed. MIND POWER instructs on how to:
- harness the powers of your mind
- tap into your creativity
- improve your self-image
- interpret your dreams
- heal yourself
- develop a "prosperity consciousness"

John Kehoe, author of MIND POWER, lecturer and philanthropist, has been teaching people the astounding powers of the mind for nearly twenty years. He first developed his MIND POWER program in 1978, following a four year seclusion in the woods of the Pacific Northwest. Since then he has taught hundreds of thousands of people around the globe. Kehoe will be touring in Dallas on Wednesday, June 4 and Thursday June 5 and is available for interview.

He was everything his press release promised. He explained the power of dreams to solve problems and then dozed off on-camera, so that we could show how he earns his paycheck.

John *does* have a dream job. And he's so media savvy, he makes sure the reporters dream story comes true.

### ALL THE NEWS THAT'S FIT TO PRINT

When sending a press release, it's seldom a bad idea to include a copy of a newspaper article that's been written on your story. It's another way of saying, "Hey, it's already been in the news somewhere else, so obviously other discerning journalists consider it a story."

When Bob Golub, a comic from New York, was in town trying to get publicity for his appearance at a local comedy club, he sent an article along with his press release. The article had been printed in papers from coast to coast about a gimmick Bob had developed on the streets of New York. He sells "lucky" potatoes.

The Associated Press article began, "In the megabucks world of Wall Street, Bob Golub trades in small potatoes; the brown, bumpy kind for a dollar a piece. But your buck gets you more than an uncooked meal in a peel, insists Golub, who spins stories to pin-striped passers-by about how his special spuds will bring them luck."

I didn't need to read any further. I could instantly see Bob trying to sell his lucky spuds on the streets of Dallas and the funny reactions we could capture on camera. But to be honest, seeing it published in the paper gave the story even more *a-peel*. This wasn't just some nut hawking hash browns, I concluded. If it was good enough for the AP, it was good enough for me.

### NEXT TIME SEND CREAM-FILLED

I can always tell when another Krispy Kreme doughnut shop is opening in our area, because the company will deliver four or five dozen doughnuts to the newsroom the day before. Is Krispy Kreme buying the story?

No. But they sure have bought our attention. The doughnuts usually last only a few minutes as employees from all over the station descend on the newsroom. And never once have I seen an unopened box of doughnuts in the trash next to the fax machine along with all the other discarded news releases we received that day.

## I'll Drink to That

One of my favorite press releases of all time announced the arrival of the "World's Leading Beer Taster." He was an expert on beers who was on tour promoting his book, *The Beer Hunter*. Well, the public relations firm promoting his appearance sent me a press release covered in bottle caps. There were probably 100 bottle caps from every imaginable beer glued to the press release. It got my attention. I covered the story. And afterwards, I called up the PR person who came up with the idea to congratulate her on the most creative press release I had ever read. In case you're wondering, she didn't have to consume all those beers to make that masterpiece. Her local bar had provided her with all the "arts and crafts" materials she needed.

That's not to say sending stuff guarantees coverage. We'll gladly consume your pizzas without sending a photographer to the ribbon-cutting of your new Italian restaurant. However, sending visuals or edibles never hurts. And if anyone with Krispy Kreme is reading this, the guys up in engineering want to know when to expect your next press release.

## The Fear of Getting Scooped

But of all the tips I've given you on getting our attention, this one may be the most important. There is no greater fear in the world of journalism than the fear of getting beaten on a story. If reporters think everyone else is going to cover it and scoop them, you won't be able to find enough parking spaces for all the media.

My wife gets dozens of calls a week from people begging for coverage on her entertainment segment. "Just the mention of another station possibly doing a story takes me from casually interested to how-soon-can-we-get-there interested," Victoria says. "It doesn't matter whether the other stations actually show up or not. It's the fear of being the only one not doing the story that puts me in a panic."

Now, don't get me wrong. No one is suggesting that you lie to get us to come out and cover your story or event. But believe me, it wouldn't hurt your cause one bit to mention either on the phone or in the cover letter of your fax that the other stations have shown an interest and you thought that it was only fair to make sure we had the story too.

"Didn't want to leave you out," is an expression that always gets my attention. And it will have me racing over to my bosses to let them know that if we don't jump on the story, we'll probably see it on the other channels first or in the newspaper the next day.

## NEWS YOU CAN USE

- Watch, read, and study the news so you know who ya gonna call.
- Start with praise. "Jeff, I loved that turkey story you did last week," beats just about any opening line you could use. It puts the reporter in the right frame of mind for your pitch. It's like a baseball player setting up his fastball with a curve.
- Leave a thirty-second voicemail message. Any longer and it's a good candidate to be automatically deleted.

- Go ahead and throw the fastball; one sentence that sums it up the way the anchor would lead in.
- Conserve paper. Reporters don't want to read a long press release. One page is plenty.
- Be creative. Write the press release with a headline that you can imagine appearing in the paper and write the copy as if it was going to be read on the air.
- Send along an article. It gives you more credibility. Bob Golub, the lucky potato salesman, sent along a clipping from a newspaper, and it made him look like a spud stud.
- Send visuals or, better yet, edibles. You can't buy us with doughnuts, and for goodness sakes don't feel bad if we gobble up your goodies and never send a camera. But there's nothing wrong with a little food for thought to get our attention.
- Introduce the idea of competition. "Your competitor expressed an interest," may be the most powerful phrase you can add to any sales pitch. One of the most motivating forces on earth is the fear factor.

# ONE STOP SHOPPING

### MAKE IT EASY ON THE REPORTER

Reporters are no different from anyone else. Many of us are lazy. And worse, we're usually on deadline. We show up at 2:30 in the afternoon and need to have a live report at 5:00. So, you should create a story that is onestop shopping.

### EVERY DOG HAS HIS DAY

I received a call from a company that designs clothes for dogs, and they wanted me to do a story on their new line. Great story, right?

Yes, but only if the company supplies the doggie models. You can't do a story on dog duds, if you don't see them on the canine consumer. And no reporter wants to hassle with trying to find dogs for the catwalk.

No worries. This company had its act together. "Jeff, come on over. We'll have a photo session with three dogs who can model a dozen different outfits—from biker jackets to fake furs." One-stop shopping. All I had to do was show up. Once again, instant story—just add reporter.

To increase your chances of getting coverage, make it as easy as possible for the journalist. Ask yourself what elements the reporter will need to tell a story. What visuals will the media

like? What interviews will they need? Can you bring it all together at one location, or will the journalist have to run all over town to collect all the elements for a story? Believe it or not, that's how we think.

If we have to have a story on the air in a few hours, there's no time to waste. So, if forced to choose between two stories to cover, even if the more difficult one is a little better story, most reporters on deadline will choose the easier one every time.

### News Conference or Snooze Conference?

This brings me to the topic of press conferences, which can be a source of one-stop shopping when conducted correctly. But to be honest, most reporters dread press conferences.

Why? They're artificial events. You bring the media together in one place to announce something to everyone at the same time. News conferences rarely involve anyone other than the news media and the newsmaker. Yawn! Besides, the visuals are usually nonexistent. And the interview is typically with a public official or some newsmaker not directly affected by the announcement. Sorry folks, but news conferences hardly ever make great TV.

There are the exceptions of course. Sometimes a story is so big visuals don't matter. When Michael Jordan announced he was hanging up his basketball shoes to try baseball, Mike on the mike was more than enough.

But those types of news conferences are rare. Most of the time, it's just some person at a podium. It's what we in the media call "a talking head."

So how do you go about jazzing up a press conference, should you decide to hold one? First of all think visually. What's the most picturesque place you could hold a news conference? You might want to consider holding it outside—weather permitting—against a backdrop that reinforces whatever you are announcing.

Most politicians have become very good at this. When candidates want to talk about poverty, do they hold their news conference in a ballroom at the Ritz? No. They go to a slum and make their announcement against a backdrop of dilapidated buildings. In 1987 when then Vice-President George Bush wanted to trash Governor Michael Dukakis' environmental record, he went straight to Boston Harbor.

And how many times do you see the President with the American flag over his shoulder? It's not a coincidence.

In fact, Leslie Stahl from CBS News likes to tell the story about how she did a scathing report on President Reagan. She pulled clips from a dozen different speeches to make her point about how the great communicator was communicating one thing and doing another.

Stahl says after the report aired, she waited for the phone to ring in her White House cubicle. She just knew Reagan's press secretary was going to chew her out.

But when the call finally came, she was stunned when the press secretary thanked her. "Did you guys even watch the report?" Stahl asked in disbelief. Yes, they had seen the story. But they pointed out that pictures speak louder than words. They knew Stahl's words would be quickly forgotten, while the pictures of President Reagan with all those flags and cheering crowds would be remembered for a long, long time.

## A Room with a View

I can't tell you how many times I've been at news conferences where the podium was set up right in front of a window. The public relations people think they're providing a great backdrop. "Look at the beautiful skyline in the background," some will say. "That should make for a great shot."

But the people who do this have obviously never run a camera. When the background is too bright, as in the case of a window, the person at the podium will look like a silhouette. Photographers have to blast the subject with lights just to compensate for the sunlight pouring in from behind. And it's very hard to compete with the sun.

The same holds true of events held outside. Try and use the sun, don't fight it. Move your podium so the sun is casting light on your subject. Or if it's a very hot day, hold the event in the shade. But remember. The bright background rule still applies. Holding your press conference under a tree with a white, sunlit building in the background is as bad as holding it indoors against a window.

## FIND SOME REAL PEOPLE

For reporters, no story is worse than one without any ordinary people in it. Remember, politicians, public officials, and business leaders are not real people as far as the press is concerned. Real people are the folks affected by whatever the politician, public official, or business leader is talking about.

Therefore, if you want to hold a press conference that won't send the media scurrying to find real people on the street, invite some ordinary folks to the press conference and introduce them at the podium.

I covered an anti-death penalty news conference once. After leaders of the movement spoke out against executing the mentally retarded, they welcomed the parents of one such death row inmate to the microphone. His parents' words weren't nearly as eloquent as the carefully polished press release, but their tears were real.

So which do you think made the news that night? The parents were so powerful they made every single newscast. And to be honest, had the parents not been invited, the story might not have made air at all. The media might have dismissed it as just another talking-head news conference.

## BRING PROPS

Ross Perot is famous for bringing charts to his interviews. *Saturday Night Live* even started making fun of him for it. But the truth is, the Texas billionaire knew what he was doing. Especially when tackling difficult topics, such as economics, anything you can bring to make your point more understandable is a very good idea.

In fact, the best news conferences don't feel like a news conference at all. When the American Trucking Association wanted to promote driver safety, they called a news conference. But there was no podium, no formal statement, just trailer trucks with drivers prepared to take reporters and photographers out on the road.

We all got the same story at the same time. But we conducted our interviews while the trucker was driving, and our audience saw how inconsiderate some motorists are to truckers. Why have a trucker tell his story from behind a podium when he can show it to you from behind the wheel?

## NEWS YOU CAN USE

- Make it easy for reporters. One-stop shopping increases your chances of getting coverage.
- Don't be boring. Choose interesting locations to put your story in the right light.
- Find real people, such as the trucker, to help drive home your message
- Show and tell isn't just for kindergarten. The more you show, the better the chances are that we'll tell your story.

# BECOMING AN EXPERT

### You Don't Need a Diploma

We've all seen people giving advice on the news and said to ourselves, "What makes them experts?" Well, I'm about to let you in on a little known secret: They're on TV.

When the news crowns you with the title "expert," you are one. And how do we decide who is and isn't one? Do we require your résumé, references, and report cards from grade school? Nope. We use the term "expert" very loosely.

The truth is, all of us are experts on something. Have a large rare coin collection? You're an expert on coins. Eat out a lot? You're a restaurant critic. Handy with hammer? You're an expert on home repair. See what I mean?

### The Plane Truth

Texas travel agent Tom Parsons has become a national expert on the airline industry. It all started in the early '80s when he began giving radio and TV interviews about the ticket bargains the airlines don't like to talk about. And Parsons probably hasn't turned down a media request since. Today, his small one-room travel agency has grown into a nationally-known discount travel company, Bestfares.com, which takes up several floors of an Arlington office building. "And you know what?" Tom said with pride. "I've never spent a nickel on advertising."

How did he do it? Well, whenever Dallas reporters need a quote on anything related to the airline industry, we all know that Parsons is ready with an answer. He'll talk about everything from flight delays to how a recent merger will effect fares.

In fact, he's so accommodating to us he's practically the only airline expert in my Rolodex. Why? It's because he never, ever turns down an interview. And if he doesn't have the answer when you call, he'll have one by the time you get to his office.

He's such a reliable source of information that, now, even the national news media have discovered him. He often appears on the network morning shows and is regularly quoted in the largest newspapers in the nation. But radio is where Parsons really works his magic. He does so many radio interviews these days, he had a studio microphone and special radio-ready phone line installed at home, so he sounds like he's actually at the radio station.

Every day before he heads for work, he spends about an hour talking to DJs and radio reporters all over the country. And every time he's interviewed he mentions Bestfares.com, which drives more people to his Web site.

## SOME EXPERT ADVICE

There are thousands of travel agents in this country and yet, Parsons is the one getting most of the free publicity.

Want some expert advice? If you know a lot about something, become an expert, and use it to your advantage. TV morning shows and radio hosts all over the country are dying for segments to fill time. Give them a hand.

Think hard. What are you an expert in, and how can you develop that expertise into something that would be good TV, radio, or newspaper?

## BOUNCING BABIES

A couple of moms from Denver have become nationally known fitness gurus all because of one very simple idea. Deidre Halacy Byerly and Lisa Stormes Hawker became frustrated with all the fitness videos that were on the market. They all seemed to feature beautiful models working out in thongs. "Who looks like that?" the mothers asked themselves. "And besides, who has kids who will leave them alone long enough to work out?"

So they hatched an idea. Why not make their own video and hold their babies while they exercised? Not only was this a unique form of resistance training, but it made for a really cute video. These moms cradled their babies in their arms while doing squats and lifted them over their heads while working their shoulders. There were no models in this video, only real workouts for real mothers.

The ladies started marketing their video by getting free publicity in the Denver media. And soon they discovered they had a hit! The media loved them. Before they knew it, they were on cross-country tour, appearing on TV stations from New York to New Mexico.

What made them experts on fitness? Nothing, really. They had kids and had figured out how to do exercises with them. Just being on the air gave them all the credibility they needed. And every newspaper article printed about them became part of the press packet they handed to the next reporter covering their story.

## DRESSED FOR SUCCESS

Dana Mayeux of Dallas learned long ago she had an eye for fashion and a mouth to match. "I've always been able to tell what colors and styles work for people, and I have to bite my tongue when I see someone wearing something that just doesn't work!" So Dana decided to become a professional image coach. She knew turning her fashion sense into dollars and cents wouldn't be easy. She had to establish herself as an expert.

She started by volunteering to teach an adult education class on the subject. As a former model and school teacher, she had no problem being approved to teach others about image.

Then, using the class to establish her credentials, she began booking herself on the local TV morning shows. She went from station to station giving the anchors on-air wardrobe advice. And the viewers loved it. Before she knew it, she was appearing on network news programs. She had arrived!

But she didn't stop there. Dana wrote a book called *101 Image Inspirations*, knowing that the book would give her even more credibility. Now there is no question that Dana is an image expert. Just look at what she did to reshape her own.

## OPPORTUNITY KNOCKS

Opportunity for free publicity is banging at your door every day, but most of us aren't listening for it. Read the paper, watch TV news, and listen to the radio. Are they talking about something that you know a lot about? Call in and offer your "expert" advice.

Suppose you run a car repair business, and the rising price of gas is in the news. There's an opportunity for free publicity. Call the local TV stations and offer to help with a segment. Outline how you could give viewers cost-cutting tips to save money on fuel, from keeping tires properly inflated to changing the oil to debunking the myths about super-unleaded gas versus regular unleaded.

Or let's say it's tax season and you're an accountant. Tell the stations you'd like to help with a segment called "The Top Ten Things Most People Forget to Deduct." They'll probably take you up on it because most accountants want only publicity when they have time (i.e. after tax season, when the media isn't interested!) Tell them you'll bring props into the studio to keep the segment from being just a bunch of "talking heads."

Who knows? You just might be so good that a station will offer you a regular weekly segment on your area of expertise. Just flip the channels. Every TV morning show brings in guests to fill time. How do you think all those doctors, fitness instructors, and fashion experts got on those shows? Don't wait for the media to find you.

## NEWS YOU CAN USE

- Use your expertise for free publicity. Everyone is an expert on something.
- Be available. As I said in the last chapter, reporters are lazy. We'll go back to the same sources over and over again as long as they deliver.
- Jump on items that are in the news. The media will be more excited to talk to you if you're trying to lend your expert help to a story they are already working on.

# SOUND BITE MACHINE

### TALKING THE TALK

Every once in a while, reporters run into someone who has a silver tongue, a person whose every sentence is a ready-to-print quote. But these folks are rare. Most of the time, a good quote is a happy accident. It doesn't have to be that way.

You, too, can become what's known in our profession as a sound bite machine. In this chapter, I'll help you master the art of the seven-second sound bite. You don't have to run out and buy a stopwatch. There's no magic to my seven-second rule. I just know after twenty years of putting together television pieces, that the best quotes are those pithy little sentences that seem to sum everything up. In fact, bells go off in my ears whenever someone delivers one. We may interview you for an hour on tape, but all we're really interested in are those seven-second gems. Honestly, as soon as I hear one, I say to myself, "No more calls, we have a winner!"

## FREEZING TIME

I'll give you an example. I was reporting on cryonics hoping to answer the question "Why would anyone want to get frozen at the moment of death, when you have no way of knowing whether science will ever be able to bring you back?"

My feature focused on Jim Halperin of Dallas. In addition to owning Heritage Rare Coin Galleries, the world's largest rare coin company, Halperin is the author of several books, including *The First Immortal*, a critically-acclaimed novel on the subject of cryonics. It was while doing research for his book that Halperin became convinced that cryonics is possible, so he signed up for it himself.

Now, you should understand that Halperin is a very logical businessman. He makes critical decision on the value of coins, often involving a small fortune, everyday. So why would such a man sign up for a service that offers no guarantees? "Well, I figure it's a lot better odds than letting the worms eat me," Halperin told me on camera.

Wow! What a sound bite! He summed up all his knowledge on the subject in one punchy little sentence. He could have said, "Cryonics isn't as final as being buried." But that wouldn't have had nearly the impact. As far as I know Halperin has never been coached in the art of delivering quotes. He's just a natural. But there's no reason you can't become a sound bite machine too.

## DARE TO PREPARE

It's amazing how many people beg me to do a story about them, yet have never given a moments thought to what they might say once the camera starts rolling. Believe it or not, most reporters don't have a hidden agenda. We're not trying to twist your words or make you say something you don't want to say. All we are trying to do is tell the story while being both informative and entertaining. You can help us by preparing for the interview.

What are the points you'd like to make? What questions do your friends ask you about the subject? If you give the interview enough thought, you won't be surprised by anything the reporter asks.

In fact, if you've crafted some great quotes beforehand, you can always answer a difficult question the way many politicians do: "That's an excellent question, and it reminds me of another point I'd like to make." Then you change the subject and deliver answers to the questions you've already thought about.

### PUTTING SOME TEETH INTO YOUR SOUND BITES

The best sound bites are rarely informational. They serve only one purpose: to add flavor to the story. In other words, the reporter prepares the meal, and you add the spice.

Just think about the memorable quotes from political debates over the years. We remember Walter Mondale asking "Where's the beef?" We remember Ronald Reagan saying, "There you go again." And we remember Lloyd Bentson scolding Dan Quayle, "I knew Jack Kennedy. Jack Kennedy was a friend of mine. You're no Jack Kennedy."

None of those quotes are very informative. They are just zingers. And don't think for one moment those quotes were ad-libs. Each candidate's writers and coaches carefully crafted them. You don't have to be Walt Whitman, or even Walt Mondale, to come up with some great quotes of your own.

### HERE'S HOW

Some of the best sound bites I've ever heard are analogies—parables, if you will—to prove a point. For instance, I interviewed a woman about her pothole problem. For years, the city had failed to fix the craters in front of her house. And when she learned that the city was about to spend $70 million on an extravagant bridge, she said on camera, "It's like having a run-down house and buying new furniture." Boy, did the bells go off in my head when she delivered that little beauty! I didn't need to ask her anything else. End of interview. She couldn't have summed up her feelings any better if she had talked for days. It was the perfect seven-second soundbite.

## Clever Endeavor

If you're clever, you can turn an otherwise boring statement into a great sound bite. Mondale could have said, "There's no substance." Instead, he played off a popular Wendy's commercial that was running at the time and his "Where's the beef?" remark became one of the most memorable quotes of his campaign. Quotes drawn from pop culture make great sound bites, and there's no debating that.

Use colorful and descriptive words. Jim Halperin's "better odds than letting the worms eat me" was a pretty vivid way of describing what happens when you're six-feet under. Maybe being frozen wouldn't be that bad, after all.

Don't be afraid to use slang for effect. Baseball legend Yogi Berra may be best known for having said, "It ain't over till it's over." No, it wasn't proper grammar. But something tells me he wouldn't have become the icon he is, if he didn't take some liberties with his language. And there ain't nothing wrong with that!

## Examples

Don't say: "I hope the Yankees win."

Say: "The Yankees will beat the Dodgers like a short-order cook beats eggs."

Don't say: For a while I struggled to build my business.

Say: "When I first started, I was so broke I used to go to weddings just for the rice!"

Don't say: "It's just about over."

Say: "The fat lady ain't singing yet, but I can hear her clearing her throat."

Got the idea? If you dare to prepare, you can come up with a clever way of saying just about anything. And trust me, if your quote is well-crafted, it'll be the one the media uses.

## WATCH THE JARGON

Doctors have a really tough time with this. They say, "lacerations and contusions" when they should say, "cuts and bruises." Never forget your audience. Most people you reach through the media didn't go to medical school. You can be authoritative and still be conversational. Avoid technical words, and replace them with words that even someone who knows nothing about your subject will understand.

The same goes for numbers and statistics. Numbers are fine and they have their place, but most will be lost on people unless they can see them. If the figure is 52 percent, say "a little more than half." And it's even better when you can make the number relevant to someone's life. If you're criticizing a government project as being too expensive, don't say $10 million. Say: "We could buy 15 million hot lunches for needy schoolchildren with the money we're spending on this lame project."

## NEWS YOU CAN USE

- Great sound bites aren't happy accidents. Just ask Mondale's speech writer.
- Use analogies to make your point. "Old house, new furniture" is just a better way of saying "bad roads, new bridge."
- Use colorful language. "Worms eating you" is much better' than just saying "buried."

- Slang is fine when it's clear you are using it on purpose. It can make you seem more conversational and folksy.
- Avoid technical talk. Everyone at your office may understand you, but Joe six-pack on the couch won't have a clue.

# MIKE WALLACE IS HERE TO SEE YOU

### HANDLING NEGATIVE NEWS

Anyone who ever watched Mike Wallace grill someone on *60 Minutes* knows how hot that fire can be. But you don't have to go hiding under your desk at the first sign of a crisis.

The truth is most reporters aren't like Mike. We're not trying to trip you up so we can barbecue you on the six o'clock news. Most of us just want to get a balanced story together in time for air.

Negative news happens. The question becomes, "How do you deal with the media to make sure an already bad story doesn't get worse?"

The patterns of responses to negative news can be broken down into categories. And these approaches are all too familiar to working journalists.

## THE OSTRICH

As the name suggests, this person sticks his head in the sand and hopes the story will go away. Bad idea. Stories don't go away; they just go on without you. Instead of having someone from the company responding to help balance the report, the reporter ends up standing in front of your building staring at the camera and saying something like, "The company refuses to comment."

I've never understood why organizations would pass up an opportunity to explain what happened. All they're doing is forcing the reporter to search for other people to interview, such as neighbors, employees, and people on the street who may or may not have facts.

The story will unfold with or without you. Trust me, you're usually better off being a part of the story than not.

## DENY, DENY, DENY

This is another favorite reaction to negative news. It's the "when in doubt, deny" approach. President Clinton used it for about two years in fighting off allegations of sexual impropriety with Monica Lewinsky. Who can forget the now infamous words "I did not have sex with that woman, Ms. Lewinsky"?

Well, I guess denial will work if you truly did nothing wrong or if you know for sure that the media will never, ever discover the truth. Unfortunately for the guilty, sooner or later the real story almost always comes out. We in the media are like sharks. If we smell blood, we'll keep circling. President Clinton can attest to that. Following his first denials of the affair, every news conference or public appearance included some shouted questions about the scandal. Wouldn't he have been much better off just coming clean when the scandal first broke?

The public is very forgiving. We all make mistakes. But we're seldom so understanding when we catch someone lying to us.

## HALF-TRUTHS

This strategy isn't much better than an outright denial. It's the "I didn't inhale" approach.

Remember Vanilla Ice? He became an overnight sensation as a white rap artist with his hit Ice, Ice, Baby. The press release his publicists sent to reporters said he grew up in the ghetto. But when word leaked out that he was actually raised in an affluent suburb of Dallas, Ice was in hot water.

When confronted with the discrepancy, he didn't do enough to distance himself from the inaccuracy. Ice's career began to melt down. He's now regularly featured on VH1 in a popular segment about fallen stars. When asked what he would have done differently, Vanilla Ice now admits he wishes he'd just come clean.

## HONESTY

Which brings me to the final category. This is the "fess up" strategy. The irony is, even though it's the most effective way to deal with negative news, it seems to be the least often used.

In the late '80s, reporting in Lincoln, Nebraska, I was assigned to cover politics, and at the time Bob Kerrey was governor. He held a weekly news conference and took questions about whatever issue happened to be in the news. One week the story that everyone was talking about was how the governor had suddenly switched his position on a bill before the legislature.

A few minutes before the news conference was to begin, the reporters made an informal alliance. We vowed not to let the governor tap dance around the issue. We would keep asking follow-up questions until he admitted to the flip-flop.

As soon as Kerrey entered the room and began taking questions, we nailed him, "Governor, why did you withdraw your support from the legislation now before the Senate?" I'll never forget his answer. Never have three words let so much energy out of a room.

"Changed my mind," he said. We were stunned. We'd all prepared to gang up on him. But there was no denial. He didn't try to candy-coat anything. He had simply exercised a very human quality—changing his mind. I guess people are allowed to do that, aren't they?

He went on to explain why he had changed his mind, but even if he hadn't, the result would have been the same. I left the room that day thinking how shrewd he had been. He was honest. We hadn't counted on that. Had he denied the flip-flop, we would have been all over him for days. Instead it was a one-day story.

## What Were You Thinking?

When actor Hugh Grant was caught with a prostitute behind the back of his then-girlfriend Elizabeth Hurley, he faced a potentially career-wrecking event. Weeks before the news broke, he'd been booked as a guest on *The Tonight Show.*

Fearing what Jay Leno would ask him, many stars would have canceled the appearance. Grant instead bravely faced the fire. "Hugh, what were you thinking?" Jay asked in disbelief. And what did Hugh do? Did he deny? Did he tell a half-truth? No, he smiled nervously and with that sheepish smile he's become famous for, said, "That's the problem. I wasn't think-ing." And the audience loved it. Hugh's relationship with Elizabeth didn't survive the scandal, but he kept his career on track by simply telling the truth.

## Apologize

When an apology is in order, do it immediately. I'm sure corporate attorneys will disagree with me on this one. Many companies are so scared of litigation, they never admit any mistakes that could come back and haunt them. But I would argue that, if your company truly messed up, there's going to be a lawsuit anyway. And how much is your corporate image worth? No jury award is as expensive as the damage you can do yourself by mishandling a crisis.

## SHOW YOUR HUMAN SIDE

Large companies can appear cold and intimidating from the outside. That's why it's so important to put a human face on any mistake.

Parkland Hospital in Dallas delivers more babies each year than any hospital in the country. But on the very same week that it was featured on *Good Morning America* as the busiest baby hospital in the nation, Parkland experienced a potential public relations nightmare.

Two infants with the same last name were delivered stillborn on the same day. A staff member mixed the names up and before the mistake was discovered, one of the families had already buried the wrong baby. The second baby was still in the morgue.

I arrived at the hospital with the family whose baby had already been buried. They wanted answers, and they wanted their baby's body exhumed as soon as possible.

While the family waited in another room, I found myself sitting across from April Foran, the public relations director for Parkland. "Jeff, I'm just heartbroken," she told me. "This is horrible. I can't imagine what that family is going through."

I made a suggestion. Since she was going to have to talk to the family in a few minutes anyway, I urged her to allow us to be there with a camera. "April, I can see the pain on your face. If you will allow me to show your compassion, to my audience, I'm sure the story will come off looking a lot better for the hospital."

What viewers saw that night on the news wasn't the cold exterior of a hospital but rather the warmth of a woman who truly felt for this family. April appeared to be almost in tears herself as she apologized to the family and promised that the hospital would do everything it could for them. The story that night was one filled with compassion thanks to April allowing us to put a human face on the hospital.

## APPOINT A SPOKESPERSON

Like April, whomever you designate as a media spokesperson should be warm, friendly, and comfortable on camera. That may sound pretty basic. But many police departments, for example, appear to do very little screening before selecting their public information officers.

Remember, your spokesperson will embody your organization. And never is that more important than in a crisis. The spokesperson should be confident, reassuring, and most of all, human.

All too often companies faced with negative news will send someone out to read a cold unemotional press release. It's understandable that you may not want your spokesperson to stray too far from the facts, especially when a crisis is still unfolding. But do yourself a favor and find someone who can speak from the heart and show compassion.

## NEVER SHOW ANGER TOWARD THE MEDIA

Anger on camera rarely plays well with the public. I know reporters aren't held in the highest esteem, but getting mad at us on camera isn't the wisest way to respond to tough questions.

I once covered a horrible accidental police shooting. An officer responding to a burglar alarm had accidentally shot the homeowner. The following day the police chief held a news conference. He started out doing everything right, showing great concern and promising that the city would do all it could to help the victim's family.

But when the questions turned to the subject of police procedure, the chief became increasingly angry. Finally after the fourth or fifth such question, the chief snapped, "That's not what we're here to talk about!" and abruptly ended the news conference.

I understood that police departments are like a family and that the chief may have felt like his family was being attacked. But in this case, he could have redirected the questions another way. Even a simple, "We'll get into that at another time; today we're too shaken up," might have worked. Instead, the chief's compassion and composure were replaced by a look that was combative.

The chief's outburst didn't fit into my story, so my viewers never saw it. Besides, I had known the chief for years and decided to give him a break. The chief had built up enough goodwill with the assembled media that I don't think anyone hung him out to dry on the news. But any one of us could have.

In fact, his outburst could have become the story, had we chosen to take that angle. Attacking the media is a poor strategy. Print reporters have an old expression: "Never pick a fight with anyone who buys ink by the barrel."

## NEWS YOU CAN USE

- Don't stick your head in the sand. The reporters will still be there when you finally come up for air.
- Denying works only when you're truly innocent.
- Half-truths leave you half-naked when the whole truth comes out.
- Honesty really is the best policy. If you mess up, 'fess up. Apologize and move on.
- Don't be afraid to show your human side.
- Appoint a spokesperson who's comfortable on camera.

- Never show anger, even when you're being attacked. It just doesn't play well on camera. The audience will decide if the reporters are being too tough. It's much better to play the victim of a hostile media instead.

# IT'S SHOW TIME!

Okay, you've charmed the media into giving you coverage. And they can't eat even one more Krispy Kreme. What do you do once that red light illuminates and you're on the air? Where do you look? What do you say? What if your mind goes blank and you freeze up? Worse yet, what if the reporter making friendly chit-chat with you just seconds before air decides to pull a "Mike Wallace" on you?

First of all, take a deep breath and relax. As we like to say in the newsroom, it's only television. Believe me, everything that can happen to someone on live TV has happened to me. I've frozen up. I've stumbled through live reports. One time I even forgot my name. But you know what? Life went on. I didn't lose my job. They didn't take my house away. I learned from my mistakes, and I improved. You will too.

## LOOKING COMFORTABLE ON CAMERA

The number one fear in America is public speaking. And because television reaches so many more people than could fit into even the largest auditorium, people always ask me how I can seem so comfortable on TV with so many people watching.

But the truth is, when I'm on camera all I see is a lens and a photographer. Most of the time there's no one else around. And I try not to think too much about how many people are watching at home. Even veteran reporters can scare themselves into looking nervous on camera if they begin obsessing about the number of viewers or what would happen if they suddenly froze up.

Concentrate on talking to the reporter or anchor conducting the interview. And if you do freeze up, so what? If what you are talking about isn't too serious, laugh at yourself and plow ahead.

## WHERE DO I LOOK?

This is a common problem. People don't know whether to look at the camera or the interviewer. I'll make it simple. Always look at the interviewer. Believe me, it will be much easier for you to keep your composure if you're not worrying about whether you are looking at the right camera. Just pretend you're having a conversation with the interviewer while the audience at home is only eavesdropping.

## PROPPING YOU UP

Bringing props to the interview is a very good idea. The media loves visuals. Props will make your television appearance more interesting and may also help you relax. You'll be illustrating your points rather than trying to make an impact with your mere words.

Talking heads are rarely good TV, and if your ultimate goal is to be so good you get invited back for future interviews, always strive to make your appearance as memorable as possible. Interesting props are a great way to do that.

## WHAT ABOUT RADIO?

I would encourage you to bring props even to a radio interview. So what if the audience can't see what you hold up? It still may help get the host more excited about your segment. And don't worry, most radio professionals are very gifted at describing whatever they see. Radio has long been called "Theater of the Mind" and what theater is complete without props?

## EVEN PROPS FOR PRINT?

Props are good for any medium. The bottom line is that most of us are visually oriented. If we can see it, we understand and remember it. Bring props to a newspaper interview, if for no other reason than to help the reporter tell your story. And if you're lucky, a photographer may come along. Good props make for great pictures. And great pictures mean more people will read and remember the article.

## WHAT DO I WEAR?

For television appearances, it depends on what kind of image you are trying to create. Professionals should wear suits or dresses. I've always found darker colors work best for that business look.

But let's say you're a dog trainer. If you show up in a suit you hardly look the part. Wear what you would usually wear on your job. The only cautions I would add are:

1. Avoid wearing an outfit with a fine checkered pattern. Studio cameras tend to freak out and your outfit may appear to glow on TV.
2. Don't wear anything too shiny for the same reason (i.e. lip gloss or shimmery blouses).

3.  And if the interview is outside on a bright day, a white shirt is much too bright for the camera. Trust me on this one. The photographer will thank you for wearing blue.

## WHAT DO I SAY?

The best advice is to focus only on points you'd like to make. Try to be concise. Most often you're going to get a few minutes or less. Sometimes after the story is edited, you'll wind up with only a few seconds.

Rehearse your answers. Role-play with someone. Candidates go over potential questions and answers during the weeks leading up to a big debate for a good reason. Few of us are great ad-libbers, but if you have enough time to prepare you can come up with some great lines that sound "off the cuff."

In short, never go into an interview without trying to anticipate the questions. It's fair game to ask the reporter beforehand what the topic is and what he or she hopes to get out of the interview.

It's unlikely the reporter will give you a list of questions, nor should you ask for one, but, if you really stop and think about it, you can usually guess what the questions will be. And if you don't know an answer never be afraid to say so.

## BE OPEN AND HONEST

Dallas radio host Chris Jagger says the secret to getting more airtime on his morning show is to let your guard down. "We usually will book guests for ten-minute segments," Jagger says. "But many guests will never get the whole ten-minutes, because we can tell they're not being honest. We've even cut celebrities off because they were too stiff and boring. But, if you keep things moving and you're fresh, interesting, and open, we might even keep you on for longer than ten minutes."

Don't be afraid to reveal your true self. Audiences are

drawn to honesty. It makes you real. It makes you interesting. It gets you more air time.

## DEATH OF A SALESMAN

We know why you want to be on the air. Most folks are trying to sell something. But whether you're selling a book, a product, or just trying to sell yourself, be careful not to come on too strong. Radio personality Kellie Rasberry from the *Kidd Kraddick in the Morning* show remembers when motivational speaker Tony Robbins was on the air. "He'd called to pitch his new book, and despite our best efforts to get him to talk about other things, he wouldn't stop talking about the book." Rasberry says it got so bad that host Kidd Kraddick walked out of the studio, down the hall, poured himself a cup of coffee, came back and Robbins was still talking. "He didn't even know Kidd had left the room. Then, after he was off the phone, we made fun of him for selling so hard."

The lesson? Come on too strong with your sales pitch and you may have the host and their listeners laughing at you.

## THE HOSTILE INTERVIEW

One of the most awkward moments of President George W. Bush's 2000 campaign came when a local television reporter began quizzing him on global leaders. Bush fumbled his way through several answers, looking very uncomfortable with the questions.

I'm sure after the interview Bush's advisors coached him never to go down that path again. Bush knew the reporter was trying to embarrass him, so all he had to do was deflect it with humor. He could have said something like, "You know what? I swore off pop quizzes when I graduated high school."

Or he could have done what Henry Ford once did on the witness stand when an attorney tried to embarrass him with difficult math questions. Ford simply admitted he wasn't very smart in math but was smart enough to hire a whole staff of accountants who were.

## On Live TV You Own the Air

Years ago I learned a valuable lesson watching Jesse Jackson. He had come into our studio in Lincoln, Nebraska, for a live interview. Producers budgeted just four minutes for the segment. And every time the anchors asked him about a controversial subject he would say, "That's a good question, and it reminds me of another point I'd like to make." And then Jackson would begin talking about something unrelated that *he* wanted to talk about.

Before long, the four minutes were up, and Jackson never did answer the difficult questions the anchors were posing. Now, this won't work all the time. Many anchors will interrupt and try to get you back on topic. But once again, never be afraid to say, "I don't know," or deflect the question with humor. On live TV, whether the anchor likes it or not, you own the air.

## News You Can Use

- Don't think about the number of people watching. Focus only on having a one-on-one conversation with the interviewer.
- Bring props. Whether it's radio, TV, or newspaper, visuals help drive your points home.
- Rehearse your ad-libs. Politicians do it all the time.
- Don't get ambushed by pointed questions. Keep your cool, and deflect questions with humor when appropriate.
- When you are live, you steer the conversation. Anchors are limited by time. Use that fact to your advantage.
- Be open and honest. It will endear you to the audience.

# EXTENDING YOUR FIFTEEN
# MINUTES OF FAME

You scored big with the reporter. You created the ultimate media event. You whipped up a stunt so stunning P.T. Barnum would be proud. Now what?

The fame game can be fleeting. So if you don't want to become a one-hit wonder, read on.

### BUILD RAPPORT BEFORE THE
### REPORTER HITS THE DOOR

There are a lot of names for it. Some call it building rapport; others call it schmoozing. It really doesn't matter what you call it; just do it. Reporters are human. We develop friendships with the people we do stories on, which often plays a role in whether someone gets covered year after year.

How do you do that, you ask? Just do what you would do with anyone you wanted as a friend. Be kind. Treat the reporter with respect. Be aware of our deadlines. If the reporter seems rushed, it's because we usually are. Most of us have just a few hours to get a story on the air. So do whatever you can to help speed things along.

Ask how you can help make the story better. Few of your encounters with reporters will be confrontational, so think of yourself as an assistant producer. Do what you can to help make the story the best it can be. Does the reporter need more information? Get on it. Does he or she need another interview that you didn't anticipate? Help line it up. Whatever you can do to make the reporters job easier, will pay off.

I'm not saying you need to become best pals with every reporter you run across. But treat them all with courtesy and make their experience so good they'll want to use you again.

## BE AVAILABLE

Make sure the reporter knows that you are always available. Believe me, you'll move up in the reporters Rolodex if you are available for an interview at a moment's notice.

Most reporters work on a tight deadline. When we call you for a story, most of the time it's not for tomorrow or next week. We want you to drop whatever you are doing and make time for us immediately. Tomorrow the story I'm working on now will be yesterday's news, so if you don't want to be yesterdays news as well, be available.

## BE APPROPRIATE

Nothing will destroy your relationship with a reporter faster than pitching a story that's completely inappropriate. Before you ever send out a press release, make sure you ask yourself the question, "How is this going to play with the public?"

A TV news manager told me a horror story from her days in St. Louis. During the mid-'80s when the homeless problem was in the news, a gourmet coffee company came up with a truly tasteless way to promote a new brew.

"They sent out news releases inviting the media to a local homeless shelter to get shots of the company mascot delivering coffee to the needy," she remembered. "We were shocked when we read that an actor wearing a traditional Colombian folk costume was going to ride in on a donkey to introduce the product. The news release went right in the trash. I don't think any station sent a camera."

That happened almost twenty years ago, and she still remembers it like it was yesterday. You can see how one bad publicity stunt can ruin your company's reputation with the media for years.

## Never Violate a Reporter's Trust

It's one thing to get a phone call from someone saying, "This is the greatest story you've ever heard." We're used to exaggeration, but don't lie. Trust is everything to a reporter. If we can't trust you as a source, you will no longer be a source.

Reporters are supposed to check all facts, but the truth is when we are under a tight deadline, we can't chase down the source of every statistic in a press release. Many reporters will end up quoting what you've given them word-for-word. So make sure your facts are straight. If the reporter later discovers he put bad information on the air, your credibility as a source is destroyed.

## Thank-You Notes

After the story airs or is in print, send a thank-you note for the coverage. That simple gesture goes a long way, yet it amazes me how few take the time to do it. I'd say only one out of every hundred people I put on the news ever bothers to call or write to thank me.

And it shouldn't stop there. Take an interest in the reporters and the stories they cover. Later you might want to drop them a note for no reason other than to compliment them on a good report. Let them know that you're always keeping your eye out for other good stories to give them. Every contact keeps your name in front of them and continues to build goodwill.

## GET REPORTERS CALLING YOU

Most of the time people call begging us to do a story on them. However, some people have been the source of so many great stories, I find myself calling them begging for news. Now that's the situation you want to find yourself in. When the reporters are contacting you out of the blue instead of the other way around, you've truly arrived!

## THE BUZZ ON REPORTERS

Keep in mind that many reporters are assigned specialities. In most newsrooms the beats have names like police and courts, business, investigative, and features. Find out who is covering your beat and try to establish an ongoing relationship. For instance, for much of my career my specialty has been the end-of-the-newscast "leave 'em laughing" piece.

Several years ago, I met a beekeeper named David Lister on a story. He removes bees from homes for a living. One of the first stories we did together was about his unusual car. Because he bills himself as a Beebuster, he went out and got an old ambulance like the kind used in the movie *Ghostbusters*. And his logo? You guessed it. Instead of a ghost with a slash through it, he has a crossed out bee.

It gets better. He has a cassette with the *Ghostbusters* theme that he blasts whenever he's at a stoplight, just to draw attention to his business.

Well, he's such a character and his stories are always so memorable, I'll call him once a month just to see if he has any upcoming big bee removal jobs. I've probably used David a dozen times in the last decade, and each time he's on the air, new customers keep his phone ringing for days.

And talk about thank you notes, David is so grateful for our coverage that each year at Christmas he pulls up to the station in his beemobile and delivers a few dozen bottles of honey to the staff. The honey comes from the hives of confiscated bees he keeps at home. And each bottle is labeled with David's Beebuster logo. Marketing genius? I don't know about that, but I do know he never buys advertising. He's charmed enough members of the media over the years that he doesn't need money, just honey, to keep his business buzzing.

## News You Can Use

- Build rapport with reporters. You can never have too many friends in the media.
- Make sure your stories are always appropriate. Always ask yourself, "How will this play with the public?"
- Never, ever burn a reporter with bad information.
- A thank-you note goes a long way.
- If you consistently deliver strong stories, the media will beat a path to your door.

# CONCLUSION

So, there you are. That's how sausage is made. I only hope your appetite for news coverage has increased now that you know the ingredients.

You now know what we cover and why we cover it. You know that slow news days are a gift from the PR gods, and you understand how to take advantage of our insatiable hunger during a feeding frenzy.

You understand how to make your event visual, what to say during an interview, and how to handle Mike Wallace when he comes knocking at your door.

So what are you waiting for? Go out and make news, and be so memorable that you earn a permanent place in the Rolodex of every reporter you meet.

Understand that even armed with these secrets, in news nothing is ever certain. You may have done everything you could to put together the perfect event, and then city hall burns down and not a single reporter shows up for your story. That's just the way it goes.

But if you've learned anything, it's that the Elvis turkey stories don't have to be accidents. Come up with great stories and we'll gobble them up!

# TV NEWS WEB SITES

Okay, now it's time to start doing your homework. Start with the TV stations in your hometown. Go to their Web sites and you'll find a wealth of information: phone numbers, fax numbers, addresses, e-mails, and perhaps most importantly, which reporters cover what.

ABILENE, TX
| | |
|---|---|
| KRBC-TV | http://www.krbctv.com |
| KTAB-TV | http://www.ktabtv.com |
| KTXS-TV | http://www.ktxs.com |

ALBANY, GA
| | |
|---|---|
| WALB-TV | http://www.walb.com |
| WFXL-TV | http://www.wfxl.com |

ALBANY, NY
| | |
|---|---|
| WEWB-TV | http://www.wewbtv.com |
| WMHT-TV | http://www.wmht.org |
| WNYT-TV | http://www.wnyt.com |
| WRGB-TV | http://www.wrgb.com |
| WTEN-TV | http://www.wten.com |
| WXXA-TV | http://www.fox23tv.com |

ALBUQUERQUE, NM
| | |
|---|---|
| KASA-TV | http://www.kasa.com |
| KNME-TV | http://www.knmetv.org |
| KOAT-TV | http://www.thenewmexicochannel.com |
| KOB-TV | http://www.kobtv.com |
| KRQE-TV | http://www.cbssouthwest.com |

ALEXANDRIA, LA
| | |
|---|---|
| KLAX-TV | http://www.klaxtv.com |

ALLENTOWN, PA
    WFMZ-TV    http://www.wfmz.com
ALTOONA, PA
    WTAJ-TV    http://www.wtajtv.com
AMARILLO, TX
    KAMR-TV    http://www.kamr.com
    KFDA-TV    http://www.newschannel10.com
    KVII-TV    http://www.kvii.com
ANCHORAGE, AK
    KIMO-TV    http://www.aksuperstation.com
    KTUU-TV    http://www.ktuu.com
ASHEVILLE, NC
    WASV-TV    http://www.wasv.com
    WFBC-TV    http://www.wb40.com
    WLOS-TV    http:// www.wlos.com
ATLANTA, GA
    WAGA-TV    http://www.wagatv.com
    WATL-TV    http://www.wb36.com
    WGCL-TV    http://www.wgcl.com
    WPBA-TV    http://www.wpba.org
    WSB-TV    http://www.accessatlanta.com/partners/
                    wsbtv
    WXIA-TV    http://www.wxia.com
ATLANTIC CITY, NJ
    WMGM-TV    http://www.wmgmtv.com
AUGUSTA, GA
    WAGT-TV    http://www.wagt.com
    WFXG-TV    http://www.wfxg.com
    WJBF-TV    http://www.wjbf.com
    WRDW-TV    http://www.wrdw.com
AUSTIN, TX
    KEYE-TV    http://keyetv.com
    KGBS-TV    http://www.kgbs.com

|                | |
|----------------|-----------------------------------|
| KLRU-TV        | http://www.klru.org               |
| KNVA-TV        | http://www.knva.com               |
| KTBC-TV        | http://www.fox7.com               |
| KVC-TV         | htttp://www.kvc13.com             |
| KVUE-TV        | http://www.kvue.com               |
| KXAN-TV        | http://www.kxan.com               |
| News 8         | http://www.news8austin.com        |

AUSTIN, MN

|          | |
|----------|------------------------|
| KAAL-TV  | http://kaaltv.com      |

BAKERSFIELD, CA

|          | |
|----------|------------------------|
| KGET-TV  | http://www.kget.com    |
| KERO-TV  | http://www.kero.com    |

BALTIMORE, MD

|          | |
|----------|-------------------------------|
| WBAL-TV  | http://www.wbaltv.com         |
| WBFF-TV  | http://www.foxbaltimore.com   |
| WJZ-TV   | http://www.wjz.com            |
| WMAR-TV  | http://www.wmar.com           |

BANGOR, ME

|          | |
|----------|-------------------------------|
| WABI-TV  | http://www.wabi-tv.com        |
| WLBZ-TV  | http://www.wlbz.com           |

BATON ROUGE, LA

|          | |
|----------|-------------------------------|
| WAFB-TV  | http://www.wafb.com           |
| WBRZ-TV  | http://www.wbrz.com           |
| WVLA-TV  | http://www.nbc33tv.com        |

BEAUMONT, TX

|          | |
|----------|-------------------------------|
| KJAC-TV  | http://www.kjac.com           |
| KFDM-TV  | http://www.kfdm.com           |

BEND, OR

|          | |
|----------|-------------------------------|
| KFXO-TV  | http://www.kfxo.com           |

BILLINGS, MT

|          | |
|----------|-------------------------------|
| KTVQ-TV  | http://www.ktvq.com           |
| KULR-TV  | http:/www.kulr8.com           |

BILOXI, MS
    WLOX-TV    http://www.wlox.com
BINGHAMTON, NY
    WBNG-TV    http://www.wbng.com
    WICZ-TV    http://www.wicz.com
BIRMINGHAM, AL
    WBRC-TV    http://www.wbrc.com
    WIAT-TV    http://www.wiat.com
    WVTM-TV    http://www.nbc13.com
BOISE, ID
    KCBI-TV    http://www.2online.com
    KIVI-TV    http://www.idaho6.com
    KNIN-TV    http://www.knintv.com
    KTVB-TV    http://www.ktvb.com
BOSTON, MA
    WBZ-TV    http://www.wbz.com
    WCVB-TV    http://www.thebostonchannel.com
    WGBH-TV    http://www.boston.com/wgbh
    WFXT-TV    http://www.fox25.com
    WHDH-TV    http://www.whdh.com
    WLVI-TV    http://www.wb56.com
BOWLING GREEN, KY
    WBKO-TV    http://www.wbko.com
BRIDGEPORT, WV
    WDTV-TV    http://www.wdtv.com
BRISTOL, ME
    WCYB-TV    http://www.wcyb.com
BROWNSVILLE, TX
    KVEO-TV    http://www.kveo.com
BRYAN, TX
    KBTX-TV    http://www.kbtx.com

BUFFALO, NY
    WGRZ-TV    http://www.wgrz.com
    WIVB-TV    http://www.wivb.com
    WKBW-TV    http://www.wkbw.com

BURLINGTON, VT
    WCAX-TV    http://www.wcax.com

BUTTE, MT
    KTVM-TV    http://www.ktvm.com
    KWYB-TV    http://www.abc18-28.com

CEDAR RAPIDS, IA
    KCRG-TV    http://www.kcrg.com
    KGAN-TV    http://www.kgan.com

CHARLESTON, SC
    WCIV-TV    http://www.wciv.com
    WCSC-TV    http://www.wcsc5.com
    WMMP-TV    http://www.wmmp.com
    WTAT-TV    http://www.wtat.com

CHARLESTON, WV
    WCHS-TV    http://www.wchstv.com

CHARLOTTE, NC
    WAXN-TV    http://www.gocarolinas.com
    WBTV-TV    http://www.wbtv.com
    WCCB-TV    http://www.fox18wccb.com
    WCNC-TV    http://www.nbc6.com
    WJZY-TV    http://www.wjzy.com
    WSOC-TV    http://www.gocarolinas.com
    WTVI-TV    http://www.wtvi.org

CHARLOTTESVILLE, WV
    WVIR-TV    http://www.nbc29.com

CHATTANOOGA, TN
  WDEF-TV      http://www.wdef.com
  WDSI-TV      http://www.fox61tv.com
  WRCB-TV      http://www.wrcbtv.com
  WTVC-TV      http://www.newschannel9.com
CHEYENNE, WY
  KGWN-TV      http://kgwn.cbsnow.com
CHICAGO, IL
  Chicagoland  http://www.cltv.com
  WBBM-TV      http://www.cbs2chicago.com
  WGN-TV       http://www.wgntv.com
  WFLD-TV      http://www.foxchicago.com
  WLS-TV       http://www.abclocal.go.com/wls
  WMAQ-TV      http://www.nbc5.com
CHICO, CA
  KCPM-TV      http://www.kcpm.com
  KHSL-TV      http://www.khsltv.com
CINCINNATI, OH
  WCPO-TV      http://www.cincinow.com
  WKRC-TV      http://www.wkrc.com
  WLWT-TV      http://www.channelcincinnati.com
  WXIX-TV      http://www.wxix.com
CLARKSBURG, WV
  WBOY-TV      http://www.wboy.com
CLEVELAND, OH
  WEWS-TV      http://www.newsnet5.com
  WJW-TV       http://www.fox8cleveland.com
  WKYC-TV      http://www.wkyc.com
  WOIO-TV      http://www.hometeam19.com
COLORADO SPRINGS, CO
  KOAA-TV      http://www.koaa.com
  KKTV-TV      http://www.kktv.com
  KXRM-TV      http://www.kxrm.com

COLUMBIA, MO
  KMIZ-TV       http://www.kmiz.com
  KOMU-TV       http://www.missouri.edu/~komu
COLUMBIA, SC
  WACH-TV       http://www.wach.com
  WIS-TV        http://www.wistv.com
  WLTX-TV       http://www.wltx.com
  WOLO-TV       http://www.wolo.com
COLUMBUS, GA
  WTVM-TV       http://www.wtvm.com
COLUMBUS, MS
  WCBI-TV       http://www.wcbi.com
COLUMBUS, OH
  WBNS-TV       http://www.wbns10tv.com
  WCMH-TV       http://www.wcmh4.com
  WSFJ-TV       http://www.wsfj.com
  WSYX-TV       http://www.wsyx6.com
  WTTE-TV       http://www.wtte28.com
CORPUS CHRISTI, TX
  KRIS-TV       http://www.kristv.com
DALLAS-FORT WORTH, TX
  KDAF-TV       http://www.wb33.com
  KDFW-TV       http://www.kdfwfox4.com
  KERA-TV       http://www.kera.org
  KTVT-TV       http://www.cbs11tv.com
  KXAS-TV       http://www.nbc5i.com
  KXTX-TV       http://www.kxtx.com
  WFAA-TV       http://www.wfaa.com
  TXCN          http://www.txcn.com
DAVENPORT, IA
  KWQC-TV       http://www.kwqc.com

**DAYTON, OH**

| | |
|---|---|
| WDTN-TV | http://www.wdtn.com |
| WHIO-TV | http://www.activedayton.com |
| WKEF-TV | http://www.nbc22.com |
| WRGT-TV | http://www.nbc22.com |

**DECATUR, IL**

| | |
|---|---|
| WAND-TV | http://www.wandtv.com |

**DENVER, CO**

| | |
|---|---|
| KCNC-TV | http://www.kcncnews4.com |
| KDVR-TV | http://www.fox31.com |
| KMGH-TV | http://www.kmgh.com |
| KUSA-TV | http://www.9news.com |
| KWGN-TV | http://www.wb2.com |

**DES MOINES, IA**

| | |
|---|---|
| KCCI-TV | http://www.kcci.com |
| KDSM-TV | http://www.kdsm.com |
| WHO-TV | http://www.whotv.com |
| WOI-TV | http://www.woitv.com |

**DETROIT, MI**

| | |
|---|---|
| WDIV-TV | http://www.wdiv.com |
| WDWB-TV | http://www.wb20detroit.com |
| WJBK-TV | http://www.wjbk.com |
| WTVS-TV | http://www.wtvs.org |
| WWJ-TV | http://www.wwjtv.com |
| WXYZ-TV | http://www.detnow.com |

**DOTHAN, AL**

| | |
|---|---|
| WDHN-TV | http://www.wdhn.com |
| WTVY-TV | http://www.wtvynews4.com |

**DULUTH, MN**

| | |
|---|---|
| KBJR-TV | http://www.kbjr.com |
| WDSE-TV | http://www.wdse.org |
| KDLH-TV | http://www.kdlh.com |

## DURHAM (Raleigh-Chapel Hill), NC

| | |
|---|---|
| WLFL-TV | http://www.wb22tv.com |
| WNCN-TV | http://www.nbc17.com |
| WRAL-TV | http://www.wral-tv.com |
| WRAZ-TV | http://www.fox50.com |
| WRDC-TV | http://www.upn28tv.com |
| WTVD-TV | http://www.abclocal.go.com/wtvd/ |

## EAU CLAIRE, WI

| | |
|---|---|
| WEAU-TV | http://www.weau.com |
| WQOW-TV | http://www.wqow.com |

## ELKHART, IN

| | |
|---|---|
| WSJV-TV | http://www.fox28.com |

## ELMIRA, NY

| | |
|---|---|
| WENY-TV | http://www.weny.com |
| WETM-TV | http://www.wetmtv.com |

## EL PASO, TX

| | |
|---|---|
| KCOS-TV | http://www.kcostv.org |
| KDBC-TV | http://www.kdbc.com |
| KINT-TV | http://www.kint.com |
| KTSM-TV | http://www.ktsm.com |
| KVIA-TV | http://www.kvia.com |

## ERIE, PA

| | |
|---|---|
| WJET-TV | http://www.wjettv.com |
| WICU-TV | http://www.wicu12.com |
| WFXP-TV | http://www.fox66.tv |
| WSEE-TV | http://www.35wsee.com |

## EUGENE, OR

| | |
|---|---|
| KEZI-TV | http://www.kezi.com |
| KMTR-TV | http://www.nbc16.com |
| KVAL-TV | http://www.kval.com |

EUREKA, CA
KEET-TV    http://www.keet.org
KIEM-TV    http://www.kiemtv.com
KVIQ-TV    http://www.humboldt1.com/~kviq

EVANSVILLE, IN
WEVV-TV    http://www.wevv.com
WEHT-TV    http://www.abc25.com
WFIE-TV    http://www.nbc14.com
WNIN-TV    http://www.accessevansville.org/wnin

FARGO, ND
KVLY-TV    http://www.kvlytv11.com
KXJB-TV    http://www.kx4.com
WDAY-TV    http://www.wday.com

FLINT, MI
WEYI-TV    http://www.nbc25.net
WJRT-TV    http://www.abclocal.go.com/wjrt/
              index.html

FLORENCE, SC
WBTW-TV    http://www.wbtw.com
WPDE-TV    http://www.wpde.com

FORT MYERS, FL
WBBH-TV    http://wbbhtv.com
WGCU-TV    http://www.wgcu.org
WINK-TV    http://www.winktv.com
WZVN-TV    http://www.abc7.com

FORT SMITH, AR
KFSM-TV    http://www.kfsm.com
KHBS-TV    http://www.khbs-khog.com

FORT WAYNE, IN
WANE-TV    http://www.wane.com
WKJG-TV    http://www.nbc33.com
WPTA-TV    http://www.wpta.com

FRESNO, CA
    KFSN-TV    http://www.abclocal.go.com/kfsn/
                     index.html
    KJEO-TV    http://www.47tv.com
    KSEE-TV    http://www.ksee24.com
    KVPT-TV    http://www.kvpt.org

GAINESVILLE, FL
    WCJB-TV    http://www.wcjb.com
    WGFL-TV    http://www.wgfl.com
    WUFT-TV    http://www.wuft.tv
    WOGX-TV    http://www.wogx.com

GRAND RAPIDS, MI
    WGVU-TV    http://www.wgvu.org
    WOOD-TV    http://www.woodtv.com
    WWMT-TV    http://www.wwmt.com
    WXMI-TV    http://www.wxmi.com

GREAT FALLS, MT
    KFBB-TV    http://www.kfbb.com

GREEN BAY, WI
    WBAY-TV    http://www.wbay.com
    WFRV-TV    http://www.wfrv.com
    WGBA-TV    http://www.wgba.com
    WLUK-TV    http://www.wluk.com

GREENSBORO, NC
    WGHP-TV    http://www.fox8wghp.com
    WXLV-TV    http://www.abc45.com

GREENVILLE, MS
    WXVT-TV    http://www.wxvt.com

GREENVILLE, NC (Washington-New Bern)
    WCTI-TV    http://www.wcti12.com
    WNCT-TV    http://www.wnct.com

GREENVILLE, SC (Spartanburg-Asheville)
    WLOS-TV    http://www.wlos.com
    WHNS-TV    http://www.whns.com
    WYFF-TV    http://www.wyff.com

HAGERSTOWN, MD
    WHAG-TV    http://www.nbc25.com

HANOVER, CT
    WNNE-TV    http://www.wnne.com

HARLINGEN, TX
    KGBT-TV    http://www.kgbt.com
    KMBH-TV    http://www.mcallen.lib.tx.us/orgs/KMBH
    KRGV-TV    http://www.krgv.com

HARRISBURG, PA
    WHTM-TV    http://www.whtm.com
    WHP-TV    http://www.whptv.com
    WITF-TV    http://www.witf.org
    WLYH-TV    http://www.upn15.com
    WGAL-TV    http://www.wgal.com (Lancaster)
    WPMT-TV    http://www.fox43.com (York)

HARRISONBURG, VA
    WHSV-TV    http://www.whsv.com

HARTFORD, CT
    WFSB-TV    http://www.wfsb.com
    WTNH-TV    http://www.wtnh.com
    WTIC-TV    http://www.fox61.com
    WVIT-TV    http://www.wvit.com

HASTINGS, NE
    KHAS-TV    http://www.khastv.com

HATTIESBURG, MS
    WDAM-TV    http://www.wdam.com

HELENA, MT
    KTVH-TV    http://www.ktvh.com

HONOLULU, HI
    KGMB-TV    http://www.kgmb.com
    KHON-TV    http://www.khon.com
    KHNL-TV    http://www.khnl.com
    KITV-TV    http://www.kitv.com

HOUSTON, TX
    KHOU-TV    http://www.khou.com
    KHWB-TV    http://www.khtv.com
    KPRC-TV    http://www.kprc.com
    KUHT-TV    http://www.kuht.uh.edu
    KTRK-TV    http://www.ktrk.com

HUNTINGTON, WV
    WPBY-TV    http://www.marshall.edu/wpby/index.html
    WOWK-TV    http://www.wowktv.com
    WSAZ-TV    http://www.wsaz.com

HUNTSVILLE, AL
    WAFF-TV    http://www.waff.com
    WAAY-TV    http://www.waaytv.com
    WHNT-TV    http://www.whnt19.com

IDAHO FALLS, ID
    KIDK-TV    http://www.kidk.com
    KIFI-TV    http://www.localnews8.com

INDIANAPOLIS, IN
    WISH-TV    http://www.wish-tv.com
    WRTV-TV    http://www.wrtv.com
    WTHR-TV    http://www.wthr.com
    WTTV-TV    http://www.ttv4.com
    WXIN-TV    http://www.fox59.com

JACKSON, MS
    WAPT-TV    http://www.wapt.com
    WDBD-TV    http://www.fox40wdbd.com
    WJTV-TV    http://www.wjtv.com
    WLBT-TV    http://www.wlbt.com

JACKSONVILLE, FL
    WAWS-TV    http://www.wawsfox30.com
    WJCT-TV    http://www.wjct.org
    WJXT-TV    http://www.news4jax.com
    WJXX-TV    http://www.firstcoastnews.com
    WTLV-TV    http://www.firstcoastnews.com
JEFFERSON CITY, MO
    KRCG-TV    http://www.krcg.com
JOHNSON CITY, TN
    WEMT-TV    http://www.fox39.xtn.net
    WJHL-TV    http://www.wjhl.com
JOHNSTOWN, PA
    WATM-TV    http://www.abc23.com
    WJAC-TV    http://www.citipage.com
    WTAJ-TV    http://www.wtajtv.com
JONESBORO, AR
    KAIT-TV    http://www.kait8.com
JOPLIN, MO
    KODE-TV    http://www.kode-tv.com
    KSNF-TV    http://www.ksntv.com
KALAMAZOO, MI
    WWMT-TV    http://www.wwmt.com
KANSAS CITY, MO
    KCPT-TV    http://www.kcpt.org
    KCTV-TV    http://www.kctv.com
    KMBC-TV    http://www.kmbc.com
    KSHB-TV    http://www.kshb.com
    WDAF-TV    http://www.wdaftv4.com
KINGSPORT, TN
    WKPT-TV    http://www.wkpttv.com
KNOXVILLE, TN
    WATE-TV    http://www.wate.com
    WBIR-TV    http://www.wbir.com

WBXX-TV http://www.wb20tv.com
WTNZ-TV http://www.wtnzfox43.com
WVLT-TV http://www.volunteertv.com

LA CROSSE, WI
WKBT-TV http://www.wkbt.com
WLAX-TV http://www.fox25fox48.com
WXOW-TV http://www.wxow.com

LAFAYETTE, LA
KADN-TV http://www.kadn.com
KATC-TV http://www.katc.com
KLFY-TV http://www.klfy.com

LAKE CHARLES, LA
KPLC-TV http://www.kplctv.com

LANCASTER, PA
WGAL-TV http://www.wgal.com
WHTM-TV http://www.whtm.com (Harrisburg)
WHP-TV http://www.whptv.com (Harrisburg)
WITF-TV http://www.witf.org (Harrisburg)
WLYH-TV http://www.upn15.com (Harrisburg)
WPMT-TV http://www.fox43.com (York)

LANSING, MI
WILX-TV http://www.wilx.com
WLAJ-TV http://www.wlaj.com
WLNS-TV http://www.wlns.com

LAS VEGAS, NV
KLAS-TV http://www.klas-tv.com
KTNV-TV http://www.ktnv.com
KVBC-TV http://www.kvbc.com
KVVU-TV http://www.kvvu.com

LAWRENCE, KS
KMCI-TV http://www.kmci.com

LEXINGTON, VA
    WKYT-TV    http://www.wkyt.com
    WLEX-TV    http://www.wlextv.com
    WTVQ-TV    http://www.wtvq.com

LIMA, OH
    WLIO-TV    http://www.wlio.com

LITTLE ROCK, AR
    KARK-TV    http://www.kark.com
    KASN-TV    http://www.kasn.com
    KATV-TV    http://www.katv.com
    KLRT-TV    http://www.klrt.com

LONG ISLAND, NY
    News 12    http://www.news12.com

LOS ANGELES, CA
    KABC-TV    http://www.abc7.com
    KCAL-TV    http://www.kcal.com
    KCBS-TV    http://www.cbs2.com
    KCOP-TV    http://www.upn13.com
    KMEX-TV    http://www.kmex.com
    KNBC-TV    http://www.nbc4la.com
    KTLA-TV    http://www.ktla.com
    KTTV-TV    http://www.fox11la.com

LOUISVILLE, KY
    WAVE-TV    http://www.wave3.com
    WDRB-TV    http://www.fox41.com
    WHAS-TV    http://www.whas11.com
    WLKY-TV    http://www.wlky.com

LUBBOCK, TX
    KAMC-TV    http://www.abc28.com
    KCBD-TV    http://www.kcbd.com
    KLBK-TV    http://www.klbk.com

LUFKIN, TX
    KTRE-TV    http://www.ktre.com

LYNCHBURG, VA
    WSET-TV        http://www.wset.com
MACON, GA
    WMAZ-TV        http://www.wmaz.com
MADISON, WI
    WISC-TV        http://www.wisctv.com
    WKOW-TV        http://www.wkowtv.com
    WMTV-TV        http://www.nbc15.com
MANCHESTER, NH
    WMUR-TV        http://www.wmur.com
MARQUETTE, MI
    WBKP-TV        http://www.wbkp.com
    WLUC-TV        http://www.wluctv6.com
MEDFORD, OR
    KDRV-TV        http://www.kdrv.com
    KOBI-TV        http://www.localnewscomesfirst.com
    KTVL-TV        http://www.ktvl10.com
MEMPHIS, TN
    WHBQ-TV        http://www.fox13whbq.com
    WLMT-TV        http://www.upn30memphis.com
    WKNO-TV        http://www.wkno.org
    WMC-TV         http://www.wmctv.com
    WPTY-TV        http://www.abc24.com
    WREG-TV        http://www.wreg.com
MERIDIAN, MS
    WTOK-TV        http://www.wtok.com
MIAMI, FL
    WBZL-TV        http://www.wb39.com
    WFOR-TV        http://www.wfor.com
    WPLG-TV        http://www.wplg.com
    WSVN-TV        http://www.wsvn.com
    WTVJ-TV        http://www.nbc6.com

MIDLAND-ODESSA, TX
    KMID-TV     http://www.big2.com
    KOSA-TV     http://www.cbs7kosa.com
    KWES-TV     http://www.kwes.com

MILWAUKEE, WI
    WDJT-TV     http://www.cbs58.com
    WISN-TV     http://www.wisn.com
    WITI-TV     http://www.fox6milwaukee.com
    WTMJ-TV     http://www.touchtmj4.com

MINNEAPOLIS, MN
    KARE-TV     http://www.kare11.com
    KMSP-TV     http://www.kmsp.com
    KSTP-TV     http://www.kstp.com
    WCCO-TV     http://www.wcco.com
    WFTC-TV     http://www.fox29.com

MINOT, ND
    KXMC-TV     http://www.kxmc.com

MISSOULA, MT
    KECI-TV     http://www.keci.com

MOBILE, AL
    WEAR-TV     http://www.weartv.com (Pensacola)
    WKRG-TV     http://www.wkrg.com
    WPMI-TV     http://www.wpmi.com

MOLINE, IL
    WQAD-TV     http://www.wqad.com

MONROE, LA
    KARD-TV     http://www.kard.com
    KAQY-TV     http://www.abc-11.com
    KNOE-TV     http://www.knoe.com
    KTVE-TV     http://www.region10.com

MONTEREY, CA
    KSBW-TV     http://www.theksbwchannel.com

MONTGOMERY, AL
    WAKA-TV    http://www.waka.com
    WCOV-TV    http://www.wcov.com
    WHOA-TV    http://www.whoa32.com
    WSFA-TV    http://www.wsfa.com

MUNCIE, IN
    WIPB-TV    http://www.bsu.edu/wipb

MYRTLE BEACH, SC
    WFXB-TV    http://www.wfxb.com

NASHVILLE, TN
    WKRN-TV    http://www.wkrn.com
    WSMV-TV    http://www.wsmv.com
    WTVF-TV    http://www.newschannel5.com
    WUXP-TV    http://www.wuxp30com
    WZTV-TV    http://www.wztv.com

NEW BEDFORD, MA
    WLNE-TV    http://www.abc6.com

NEW BERN, NC
    WCTI-TV    http://www.wcti12.com

NEW HAVEN, CT
    WTNH-TV    http://www.wtnh.com

NEW ORLEANS, LA
    WDSU-TV    http://www.wdsu.com
    WGNO-TV    http://www.abc26.com
    WNOL-TV    http://www.wb38.com
    WVUE-TV    http://www.fox8live.com
    WWL-TV    http://www.wwl-tv.com

NEW YORK, NY
    WABC-TV    http://www.abcnews.com/local/wabc
    WCBS-TV    http://www.cbs2ny.com
    WNBC-TV    http://www.newschannel4.com
    WNYW-TV    http://www.fox5ny.com
    WNET-TV    http://www.wnet.org

WPIX-TV     http://www.wb11.com
WWOR-TV     http://www.wwortv.com

NORFOLK, VA
WAVY-TV     http://www.wavy.com
WTKR-TV     http://www.wtkr.com
WVEC-TV     http://www.wvec.com

OAKLAND, CA
KTVU-TV     http://www.bayinsider.com/ktvu

ODESSA, TX
KMID-TV     http://www.big2.com
KOSA-TV     http://www.cbs7kosa.com
KWES-TV     http://www.kwes.com

OKLAHOMA CITY, OK
KFOR-TV     http://www.kfor.com
KOCO-TV     http://www.kocotv.com
KOKH-TV     http://www.fox25.net
KWTV-TV     http://www.kwtv.com

OMAHA, NE
KETV-TV     http://www.ketv.com
KMTV-TV     http://www.kmtv3.com
WOWT-TV     http://www.wowt.com

ORLANDO, FL
WESH-TV     http://www.wesh.com
WFTV-TV     http://www.wftv.com
WKMG-TV     http://www.mycfnow.com
WOFL-TV     http://www.wofl.com

PADUCAH, KY
WPSD-TV     http://www.sunsix.com

PANAMA CITY, FL
WJHG-TV     http://www.wjhg.com
WMBB-TV     http://www.wmbb.com

PALM SPRINGS, CA
    KESQ-TV    http://www.kesq.com
    KMIR-TV    http://www.kmir-tv6.com
PARKERSBURG, WV
    WTAP-TV    http://www.wtap.com
PASCO, WA
    KEPR-TV    http://www.owt.com/kepr
PENSACOLA, FL
    WBQP-TV    http://www.wbqp.com
    WEAR-TV    http://www.weartv.com
PEORIA, IL
    WEEK-TV    http://www.week.com
    WHOI-TV    http://www.hoinews.com
    WMBD-TV    http://www.wmbd.com
    WTVP-TV    http://www.wtvp.com
PHILADELPHIA, PA
    Comcast 8    http://www.cn8.com
    KYW-TV    http://www.kyw.com
    WCAU-TV    http://www.nbc10.com
    WHYY-TV    http://www.whyy.org
    WPHL-TV    http://www.wb17.com
    WPSG-TV    http://www.wpsg.com
    WPVI-TV    http://www.wpvi.com
    WPPX-TV    http://www.paxtv.com/wppx
    WTXF-TV    http://www.foxphiladelphia.com
    WYBE-TV    http://www.wybe.org
PHOENIX, AZ
    KAET-TV    http://www.kaet.asu.edu
    KNXV-TV    http://www.phoenix360.com
    KPHO-TV    http://www.cbsfive.com
    KPNX-TV    http://www.12news.com
    KTVK-TV    http://www.azfamily.com

PITTSBURGH, PA
> KDKA-TV    http://www.kdka.com
> WPXI-TV    http://www.realpittsburgh.com/wpxi
> WTAE-TV    http://www.wtaetv.com

PITTSBURG, KS
> KOAM-TV    http://www.koamtv.com

PLATTSBURGH, NY
> WPTZ-TV    http://www.wptz.com

PORTLAND, ME
> WCSH-TV    http://www.wcsh6.com
> WGME-TV    http://www.wgme.com
> WMTW-TV    http://www.wmtw.com
> WPXT-TV    http://www.ourmaine.com

PORTLAND, OR
> KATU-TV    http://www.katu.com
> KGW-TV     http://www.kgw.com
> KOIN-TV    http://www.koin.com
> KPDX-TV    http://www.kpdx.com

PROVIDENCE, RI
> WJAR-TV    http://www.turnto10.com
> WLNE-TV    http://www.abc6.com
> WPRI-TV    http://www.wpri.com

PUEBLO, CO
> KTSC-TV    http://www.ktsctv.org

QUINCY, IL
> KHQA-TV    http://www.khqa.com
> WGEM-TV    http://www.wgemquincy.com

RALEIGH, NC
> WLFL-TV    http://www.wb22tv.com
> WNCN-TV    http://www.nbc17.com
> WRAL-TV    http://www.wral-tv.com
> WRAZ-TV    http://www.fox50.com
> WRDC-TV    http://www.upn28tv.com

RALEIGH, NC (Cont.)
    WTVD-TV      http://www.abclocal.go.com/wtvd/
RAPID CITY, ND
    KOTA-TV      http://www.kota.rapidnet.com
RENO, NV
    KOLO-TV      http://www.kolotv.com.
    KRNV-TV      http://www.krnv.com
    KTVN-TV      http://www.ktvn.com
RICHMOND, VA
    WRIC-TV      http://www.wric.com
    WRLH-TV      http://www.fox35.com
    WTVR-TV      http://www.wtvr.com
    WWBT-TV      http://www.wwbt.com
ROANOKE, VA
    WBRA-TV      http://www.wbra.org
    WDBJ-TV      http://www.wdbj7.com
    WSLS-TV      http://www.newschannelten.com
ROCHESTER, MN
    KTTC-TV      http://www.kttc.com
ROCHESTER, NY
    WBGT-TV      http://www.wbgt.com
    WHEC-TV      http://www.whec.com
    WOKR-TV      http://www.rochestertoday.com
    WROC-TV      http://www.wroctv.com
    WUHF-TV      http://www.foxrochester.com
ROCKFORD, IL
    WIFR-TV      http://www.wifr.com
    WREX-TV      http://www.wrex.com
    WTVO-TV      http://www.wtvo.com
    WQRF-TV      http://www.fox39.com
ROCK HILL, SC
    WNSC-TV      http://www.wnsc.org

ROCK ISLAND, IL
    WHBF-TV    http://www.whbf.com
SACRAMENTO, CA
    KCRA-TV    http://www.kcra.com
    KMAX-TV    http://www.upn31.com
    KOVR-TV    http://www.kovr13.com
    KTXL-TV    http://www.ktxl.com
    KVIE-TV    http://www.kvie.org
    KXTV-TV    http://www.kxtv10.com
SAGINAW, MI
    WNEM-TV    http://www.wnem.com
SALINAS, CA
    KION-TV    http://www.kiontv.com
    KCBA-TV    http://www.kcbatv.com
    KSBW-TV    http://www.ksbw.com
SALISBURY, MD
    WBOC-TV    http://www.wboc.com
    WMDT-TV    http://www.wmdt.com
SAN JUAN, PR
    WAPA-TV    http://noticentro.coqui.net
SALT LAKE CITY, UT
    KSL-TV    http://www.ksl.com
    KSTU-TV    http://www.fox13.com
    KTVX-TV    http://www.4utah.tv
    KUTV-TV    http://www.kutv.com
SAN ANTONIO, TX
    KABB-TV    http://www.kabb.com
    KENS-TV    http://www.kens-tv.com
    KJLF-TV    http://www.mykjlf.com
    KMOL-TV    http://www.kmol.com
    KSAT-TV    http://www.clickonsat.com

## SAN DIEGO, CA

| | |
|---|---|
| KFMB-TV | http://www.kfmb.com |
| KGTV-TV | http://www.thesandiegochannel.com |
| KNSD-TV | http://www.nbcsandiego.com |
| KSWB-TV | http://www.kswbtv.com |
| XETV-TV | http://www.fox6.com |

## SAN FRANCISCO, CA

| | |
|---|---|
| KGO-TV | http://www.abclocal.go.com/kgo/ index.html |
| KQED-TV | http://www.kqed.org |
| KPIX-TX | http://www.kpix.com |
| KRON-TV | http://www.kron.com |
| KTVU-TV | http://www.bayinsider.com/ktvu/ index.html |

## SAN JOSE, CA

| | |
|---|---|
| KNTV-TV | http://www.nbc3.com |

## SAN LUIS OBISPO, CA

| | |
|---|---|
| KSBY-TV | http://www.ksby.com |

## SANTA MARIA, CA

| | |
|---|---|
| KCOY-TV | http://www.kcoy.com |

## SARASOTA, FL

| | |
|---|---|
| WWSB-TV | http://www.wwsb.com |

## SAVANNAH, GA

| | |
|---|---|
| WJCL-TV | http://www.abc22tv.com |
| WSAV-TV | http://www.wsav.com |
| WTOC-TV | http://www.wtoctv.com |

## SCHENECTADY, NY

| | |
|---|---|
| WRGB-TV | http://www.wrgb.com |

## SCRANTON, PA

| | |
|---|---|
| WBRE-TV | http://www.wbre.com |
| WNEP-TV | http://www.wnep.com |
| WOLF-TV | http://www.fox56tv.com |
| WYOU-TV | http://www.wyou.com |

**SEATTLE, WA**
- KCPQ-TV — http://www.kcpq.com
- KHCV-TV — http://www.khcvtv.com
- KING-TV — http://www.king5.com
- KIRO-TV — http://www.kirotv.com
- KOMO-TV — http://www.komotv.com
- KSTW-TV — http://www.kstw.com
- KTWB-TV — http://www.ktwbtv.com
- NW Cable — http://www.nwcn.com

**SHREVEPORT, LA**
- KSLA-TV — http://www.ksla.com
- KTAL-TV — http://www.ktal.com
- KTBS-TV — http://www.ktbs.com

**SIOUX CITY, IA**
- KCAU-TV — http://www.kcautv.com.
- KMEG-TV — http://www.kmeg.com
- KTIV-TV — http://www.ktiv.com

**SIOUX FALLS, SD**
- KDLT-TV — http://www.on-ramp.com/kdlt
- KELO-TV — http://www.kelotv.com
- KSFY-TV — http://www.ksfy.com

**SOUTH BEND, IN**
- WNDU-TV — http://www.wndu.com
- WSBT-TV — http://www.wsbt.com

**SPARTANBURG, IN**
- WSPA-TV — http://www.wspa.com

**SPOKANE, WA**
- KAYU-TV — http://www.kayutv.com
- KREM-TV — http://www.krem.com
- KXLY-TV — http://www.kxly.com

**SPRINGFIELD, IL**
- WICS-TV — http://www.wics.com

SPRINGFIELD, MA
WGGB-TV http://www.wggb.com
WWLP-TV http://www.wwlp.com

SPRINGFIELD, MO
KDEB-TV http://www.fox27.com
KOLR-TV http://www.kolr10.com
KSPR-TV http://www.kspr33.com
KYTV-TV http://www.ky3.com

ST. JOSEPH, IN
KQTV-TV http://www.kq2.com

ST. LOUIS, MO
KMOV-TV http://www.kmov.com
KPLR-TV http://www.kplr.com
KSDK-TV http://www.ksdk.com
KTVI-TV http://www.fox2ktvi.com

ST. PETERSBURG, FL
WTOG-TV http://www.wtog.com
WTSP-TV http://www.wtsp.com

STEUBENVILLE, OH
WTOV-TV http://www.wtov.com

SYRACUSE, NY
WIXT-TV http://www.wixt.com
WSTM-TV http://www.wstm.com
WTVH-TV http://www.wtvh.com

TALLAHASSEE, FL
WTLH-TV http://www.fox49.com
WTXL-TV http://www.wtxl.com

TAMPA, FL
WFLA-TV http://www.wfla.com
WFTS-TV http://www.wfts.com
WTSP-TV http://www.wtsp.com
WTVT-TV http://www.wtvt.com
WWWB-TV http://www.wb32.com

TAMPA, FL (Cont.)
    Bay News 9   http://www.baynews9.com
TERRE HAUTE, IN
    WTHI-TV   http://www.wthitv.com
    WTWO-TV   http://www.wtwo.com
TOLEDO, OH
    WGTE-TV   http://www.wgte.org
    WNWO-TV   http://www.nbc24.com
    WTOL-TV   http://www.wtol.com
    WTVG-TV   http://www.13abc.com
    WUPW-TV   http://www.wupw.com
TOPEKA, KS
    KTMJ-TV   http://www.fox43topeka.com
    KSNT-TV   http://www.ksnt.com
    KTKA-TV   http://www.NewsSource49.com
    WIBW-TV   http://www.wibw.com
TRAVERSE CITY, MI
    WGTU-TV   http://www.wgtu.com
    WPBM-TV   http://www.tv7-4.com
TUCSON, AZ
    KGUN-TV   http://www.kgun9.com
    KOLD-TV   http://www.kold.com
    KMSB-TV   http://www.kmsb.com
    KVOA-TV   http://www.kvoa.com
TULSA, OK
    KJRH-TV   http://www.teamtulsa.com
    KOKI-TV   http://www.fox23.com
    KOTV-TV   http://www.kotv.com
    KTUL-TV   http://www.ktul.com
TUSCALOOSA, AL
    WJRD-TV   http://www.wjrd7.com
TWIN FALLS, ID
    KMVT-TV   http://www.kmvt.com

TYLER, TX
  KETK-TV     http://www.region56.com
  KLTV-TV     http://www.kltv.com
UTICA, NY
  WKTV-TV     http://www.wktv.com
  WUTR-TV     http://www.wutr.com
WACO, TX
  KCEN-TV     http://www.kcentv.com
  KWTX-TV     http://www.kwtx.com
  KXXV-TV     http://www.kxxv.com
WASHINGTON, DC
  WBDC-TV     http://www.wbdc.com
  WETA-TV     http://www.weta.org
  WJLA-TV     http://www.wjla.com
  WRC-TV      http://www.nbc4dc.com
  WTTG-TV     http://www.fox5dc.com
  WUSA-TV     http://www.wusatv9.com
WATERLOO, IA
  KWWL-TV     http://www.kwwl.com
WATERTOWN, NY
  WWTI-TV     http://www.wwti50.com
WAUSAU, WI
  WAOW-TV     http://www.waow.com
  WSAW-TV     http://www.wsawtv7.com
WESLACO, TX
  KRGV-TV     http://www.krgv.com
WEST PALM BEACH, FL
  WFLX-TV     http://www.wflxfox29.com
  WPBF-TV     http://www.wpbf.com
  WPEC-TV     http://www.gopbi.com/partners/news12
  WPTV-TV     http://www.wptv.com
WHEELING, IL
  WTRF-TV     http://www.wtrf.com

WICHITA, KS
   KAKE-TV        http://www.kake.com
   KSAS-TV        http://www.ksfoxnet.com
   KSNW-TV        http://www.ksn.com
   KWCH-TV        http://www.kwch.com
WICHITA FALLS, TX
   KAUZ-TV        http://www.kauz.com
   KFDX-TV        http://www.cyberstation.net/kfdx
WILKES-BARRE, PA
   WBRE-TV        http://www.wbre.com
   WNEP-TV        http://www.wnep.com
   WOLF-TV        http://www.fox56tv.com
   WYOU-TV        http://www.wyou.com
WILMINGTON, DE
   WECT-TV        http://www.wect.com
   WSFX-TV        http://www.wsfx.com
   WWAY-TV        http://www.wwaytv3.com
WINSTON SALEM, NC
   WXII-TV        http://www.wxii.com
   WXLV-TV        http://www.wxlv.com
YAKIMA, WA
   KAPP-TV        http://www.kapptv.com
   KIMA-TV        http://www.kimatv.com
YORK, PA
   WPMT-TV        http://www.fox43.com
YOUNGSTOWN, OH
   WFMJ-TV        http://www.wfmj.com
   WKBN-TV        http://www.wkbn.com
   WYTV-TV        http://www.wytv.com
YUMA, AZ
   KYMA-TV        http://www.kyma-tv.com
ZANESVILLE, OH
   WHIZ-TV        http://www.whizamfmtv.com

# ABOUT THE AUTHOR

Jeff Crilley is an Emmy Award winning TV reporter in Dallas. In his twenty years in television news, he has made hundreds of national news appearances including CNN, CNN *Headline News*, FOX News, The Discovery Channel, *Good Morning America* and The CBS *Early Show*.

Besides the Emmy, he has been recognized by his peers with dozens of national and regional awards including, the National Headliners Award, the Edward R. Murrow Award, and the Thurgood Marshall Award.

As a general assignment reporter Crilley covers a wide range of topics from presidential elections to Spam cooking contests at the State Fair. His day-to-day news gathering experience has given him special insight into what the news covers and why.

Crilley lives in Dallas where he is married to a fellow reporter and competitor, Victoria Snee, from the WB. He is a graduate of Michigan State University with a Bachelor's Degree in Communications.

When he is not covering the news, Crilley teaches people how to get covered. He is a popular speaker on Free Publicity and is often called on to share his secrets with business groups, non-profit organizations, and college classes. To schedule him for your group or class, please visit his Web site at www.jeffcrilley.com.

# FREE PUBLICITY

If you would like to order additional copies of this book, they can be purchased online at www.jeffcrilley.com.
Or you can send this form along with your payment to:

Jeff Crilley
P.O. Box 702606
Dallas, TX 75370

Number of books:_____x $12.95         =$_____
Texas residents add 8.25% sales tax ($1.07 per book) =$_____
S&H _____x $2.50 per book         =$_____
                     TOTAL =$_____

Ship to:

Name_____

Company_____

Address_____

City_____

State/Province_____

Zip_____Country_____

E-mail_____

Payment     _____Check made payable to Jeff Crilley
                _____Visa        _____Mastercard
                _____Discover      _____American Express

Card #_____Expires_____

Signature_____